HISTORICAL MATERIALISM

HISTORICAL
MATERIALISM

V. G. AFANSAYEV

INTERNATIONAL PUBLISHERS, New York

© International Publishers Co., Inc.
Revised edition
First printing, 1987

Manufactured in the United States of America

Library of Congress Cataloging-in-Publication Data

Afanas'ev, Viktor Grigor'evich.
  Historical materialism.

Rev. translation of the 2nd pt. of: Osnovy filosofskikh znanĭi.
1. Dialectical materialism. 2. Historical materialism. I. Title.
D16.9.A4513 1987   335.4′1   87-2647
ISBN 0-7178-0637-5 (pbk.)

CONTENTS

HISTORICAL MATERIALISM

CHAPTER I

The Subject Matter of Historical Materialism

Marx and Engels revealed the dialectical-materialist character of development not only of nature but also of *society,* creating thereby the only scientific theory of social development, *historical materialism.* We shall now explain what historical materialism is.

First of all, let us ascertain the nature of the revolution made by Marxism in social theories.

1. The Rise of Historical Materialism— a Revolution in Social Theories

Thinkers long ago pondered over questions about society. How does human society develop? What are its driving forces? Are the changes in society accidental or are they dictated by necessity, by objective laws? If society's development is causally conditioned, what is the chief cause, the foundation of social life? It was natural that these and many similar questions arose. Man lives in society, is bound to it by countless threads, and cannot but take an interest in the fate of society, the ways in which it develops.

Many correct ideas about social development were expressed by scholars even before Marxism. The French 18th-century materialists, for example, asserted that man, his views and behaviour are a result of the influence of social environment. French bourgeois historians (Guizot, Thierry, Mignet) pointed to the existence of opposite classes and the class struggle in society. The British bourgeois economists (Smith and Ricardo) tried to find in economic life a basis for the existence of classes. The Utopian Socialists (Saint-Simon, Fourier and Owen) anticipated individual features of future communist society.

A big contribution to the theory of social development was made by Belinsky, Herzen, Chernyshevsky and other Russian revolutionary democrats of the 19th century. Their ideas about the role of economic life in social development, about the people as the makers of history, the irreconcilability of the class interests of the exploited and the exploiters, the class character of philosophy, literature, art, and so on, were profound for their time.

1

Nevertheless pre-Marxist *sociology* was not scientific. What were its main failings?

To begin with, prior to Marx idealism reigned supreme in sociology. The French materialists, having shown the influence of the social environment on man, erroneously regarded this environment as the product of human reason. "Ideas rule the world"—this was the epitome of their views of society.

Other pre-Marxist materialists likewise had an idealist view of society. And the unscientific nature of the idealists' views of social development is self-evident. Hegel, although he made a valuable contribution to philosophy by his ideas of historical necessity and although he attempted to view the history of mankind dialectically, ultimately arrived at the false conclusion that society is ruled by divine will. God rules the world, the realisation of his plans constitute world history. This sums up Hegelian philosophy of history.

Another shortcoming in pre-Marxist sociology also stemmed from the approach to society in an idealist way. Pre-Marxist sociologists, acting on the premise that ideas rule the world and that these ideas are fathered by outstanding individuals—kings, military leaders, scholars, etc., arrived at the wrong conclusion that these great men alone make history. They did not see the decisive role played by the working people in historical development.

Pre-Marxist sociologists also proved incapable of revealing the dialectics of the historical process. In the presentation of these sociologists history appeared as a conglomeration of unconnected facts. Being idealists they were unable to grasp the unity and interconnections of social life, the real driving forces and material sources behind historical events.

Only Marx and Engels proved capable of penetrating the nature of society and fully revealing its complex and contradictory development. They overcame the shortcomings of the old sociology and created a qualitatively new theory of social development, *historical materialism*, thereby causing a revolution in social theories.

What is the substance of this revolution?

Marx and Engels drove idealism from social science. They correctly solved the fundamental question of philosophy as applied to society and formulated the principal postulate of historical materialism: *social being determines social consciousness.*

What is social being and social consciousness?

The sphere of *social being* encompasses the material life of society, and above all people's productive activity, the economic relations between them in the process of production. *Social consciousness* is the spiritual life of people, the ideas, theories and views which guide them in what they do.

In asserting that social being is primary and social consciousness secondary, Marx and Engels acted on the premise that before people can engage in science, art, philosophy, and so on, they must get food, clothing and shelter, for which they must work, produce material wealth. From this it follows that "the production of the immediate material means of subsistence and consequently the degree of economic development attained by a given people or during a given epoch form the foundation upon which the state institutions, the legal conceptions, art, and even the ideas on religion of the people concerned have been evolved, and in the light of which they must, therefore, be explained, instead of *vice versa,* as had hitherto been the case".* Historical materialism is a genuinely scientific, *materialist* understanding of history.

Marx and Engels, by singling out from the numerous social relations the economic, production relations as the chief, decisive ones, arrived at the concept of the *socio-economic formation,* a fundamental concept of historical materialism.

The *socio-economic formation* is the totality of social phenomena and processes (relating to the economy, ideology, family, way of life, etc.) based on a historically determined mode of production. Society develops through the *natural replacement* of one socio-economic formation by another, more improved. History has progressed from the primitive-communal system to the slave-owning system, then to feudalism and to capitalism, to socialism and, finally, to the communist formation.

By creating historical materialism Marx and Engels proved that *the masses, the working people,* are the *real makers of history.* The people by their labour produce all the material wealth. The labour of millions of ordinary men and women constitutes the indispensable foundation of mankind's life and progress.

Marx and Engels overcame the metaphysical nature of the old sociology and revealed the objective dialectics of social development. Thanks to this great accomplishment history ceased to be a chaotic conglomeration of unconnected facts, and appeared as an integral and harmonious process governed by dialectical laws.

* Friedrich Engels, "Das Begräbnis von Karl Marx", Marx/Engels, *Werke,* Dietz Verlag, Berlin, 1962, Bd. 19, S. 335-336.

2. The Subject Matter of Historical Materialism

The subject matter of historical materialism is the study of society and the laws of its development.

These laws are as *objective,* i.e., independent of man's consciousness, as the laws of nature's development. Like the laws of nature, they are *knowable* and are applied by man in his practical activity. There are, however, essential distinctions between the laws of social life and the laws of nature. The laws of nature reflect the operation of blind, spontaneous forces, while the laws of social development are always manifested through people, acting as intelligent beings who set themselves definite aims and work to achieve them.

The laws of social life are studied not only by historical materialism, but also by the other social sciences: political economy, history, aesthetics, pedagogics, and so on. But all these sciences study a certain group of social phenomena, examine society from one angle, without giving an idea of the process of social development as a whole. Political economy, for example, studies the economic, production relations between people. History is concerned with society's development in different epochs and in different countries. Aesthetics is confined to the sphere of art, and so on.

In contrast to the concrete social sciences, historical materialism studies the *most general* laws of social development. As an integral part of the Marxist-Leninist world outlook, historical materialism furnishes a scientific, dialectical-materialist interpretation of phenomena of social life. It solves such important general problems of historical development as the connection between social being and social consciousness, the importance of material production in people's lives, the origin and role of social ideas and of their corresponding institutions. Historical materialism enables us to understand what role the people and individuals play in history, how classes and the class struggle arose, how the state appeared, why social revolutions occur and what is their significance in the historical process, and a number of other general problems of social development.

Not all the laws studied by historical materialism have the same sphere of operation. Some of them operate at all stages and others at particular stages of society's development. Among the former are the law of the determining role of social being in relation to social consciousness and the law of the determining role of the mode of production in society's development. Among the latter is the law of the class struggle which operates only in societies divided into hostile classes.

Historical materialism also elaborates the corresponding categories or concepts which reflect the most general and essential aspects of social development. These include "social being", "social consciousness", "mode of production", "basis", "superstructure", "social progress", and many others. Only the sum total of the laws and categories of historical materialism furnishes a single and harmonious picture of social development.

Historical materialism arose as a result of the generalisation of people's practical experience throughout history and the achievements of the social sciences, and it is absolutely inconceivable outside of them. On the other hand, without historical materialism, without a knowledge of the general laws of social development no social science can develop fruitfully. Historical materialism is the *methodological foundation* of all the other social sciences. It enables historians, economists and other scholars to find their way in the intricate maze of social phenomena and determine the place and significance of each phenomenon in social life. Knowing, for example, the basic premise of historical materialism that people play the decisive role in social development, it is possible to bring out the genuine character of a particular historical event, for instance, to ascertain the causes of the social revolution, and its motive forces, and explain the source of the strength of socialism, etc. The premise of historical materialism that society's spiritual life depends on economic, material relations between people, helps to trace the sources of various theories and views and correctly assess their role in history, particularly in revolutionary periods when the replacement of one type of economic relations by another results in the fall of old conceptions and the rise of new ones.

Knowledge of the laws of historical materialism enables us not only to understand complex social phenomena, but also to *influence* social life, to *transform* it in the interests of the working people. To transform reality on the basis of the laws of social development means to give effect to the historical necessity of mankind's progressive development. In the process of this development man gains genuine freedom. Let us examine what historical materialism understands by necessity and freedom.

3. Historical Necessity and Human freedom

Historical necessity is that which naturally follows from the *internal connection* of social phenomena and therefore, *is bound* to take place. Material production, for example, necessarily determines all aspects of social life. Social revolutions or the succession of one social order by another also take place of necessity. Today capitalism is necessarily being replaced by communism.

The proponents of religious ideology do not recognise historical necessity. They claim that the entire historical process is predetermined by divine will, and that people are mere playthings in the hands of providence. The Bible says that without God's will not a single hair will fall from man's head.

In distorting the essence of social development and rejecting historical necessity, many sociologists go to the other extreme and advocate subjectivism, the reign of arbitrary will in social activity. In their opinion, the behaviour or actions of people are determined by their subjective wishes and concepts. At the same time bourgeois sociologists accuse Marxists of fatalism, of worshipping historical necessity and claiming that man is impotent in the face of social laws.

The ideologists of the bourgeoisie will not agree that historical necessity, far from precluding, presupposes people's conscious activity. Men are unable to abolish the laws of social development or to create new laws, but they are capable of understanding these laws and historical necessity, and, through being aware of necessity, to actively intervene in the socio-historical process. Practical experience has conclusively shown that, by understanding objective necessity, people subordinate not only the laws of nature to their will, as witnessed by the achievements of modern science and technology, but also the course of social events. *It is knowledge of objective necessity and its employment in the interest of man that constitute human freedom.*

Freedom does not abolish objective necessity, it signifies that man understands necessity and exploits it for his own ends. Man's activity is only free when it corresponds to objective necessity and his freedom consists not in imaginary independence from the laws of nature and society, but in knowledge of these laws and the ability to make them serve human needs.

Freedom is the result of prolonged historical development. As science and production progressed man began to bring nature under his control, learned its objective laws and thereby gradually subordinated necessity operating in nature to his will and became free in relation of nature. Man's domination over nature, however, does not give him control over social processes. Historical necessity, the law-governed development of pre-socialist societies, acted as a spontaneous force which people were unable to control. Under capitalism, for example, the law of anarchy and competition makes man a pawn in the hands of chance and dooms to failure his attempts to plan his activity in advance.

It is only socialism that for the first time creates the possibility of mastering historical necessity and achieving genuine freedom. The socialist revolution makes public ownership predominant and removes class antagonisms, as a result of which people become able to consciously direct the economic, political, and cultural life of society. With the victory of socialism society makes a tremendous leap from the kingdom of necessity into the kingdom of freedom. Moreover, as socialist society advances to communism, man's freedom becomes wider and more diverse, his domination over nature and the social processes grows, and he learns voluntarily and consciously to combine his personal interests and aspirations with the lofty ideals of society.

An indispensable condition for the growth of genuine freedom in society is the conscious productive and political activities of the people, based on the knowledge and competent application of Marxist-Leninist theory.

The Marxist-Leninist theory of necessity and freedom has been applied in the Soviet Union. Real freedom—mankind's age-old dream—has struck root here finally and irrevocably. It has been attained as a result of the triumphant socialist revolution, the heroic labour and selfless effort of the Soviet people headed by the Communist Party. Having become masters of their country, having understood historical necessity, the Soviet people gained an opportunity to make their own history consciously and purposefully.

The attainment of freedom under socialism, however, does not rule out the operation of historical necessity, of objective laws. Under socialism, too, necessity constitutes the objective basis for man's free activity, and objective laws operate, but these laws are consciously used by the Soviet people, who under the guidance of the party and the Government are fulfilling the greatest historical necessity and are building communist society.

4. The Unscientific Nature of Contemporary Bourgeois Sociology

Historical materialism, the only scientific theory of social development indicating man's true road to a better future, is hated by the reactionary bourgeoisie and its ideologists. Gripped with fear of the future and unable to check the advance of mankind to communism, the bourgeoisie seeks at least to retard historical progress and prolong the existence of the capitalist system. To this end the bourgeoisie and its ideologists resort to all possible means—economic, political and ideological. Contemporary bourgeois sociology holds an important place among their ideological weapons.

There is an endless number of trends and schools of this sociology but they all stem from the same idealistic and metaphysical root.

Renunciation of the Objective Laws of Social Development

The most characteristic feature of contemporary bourgeois sociology is the rejection of the objective laws of social development. This rejection assumes the most diverse forms in different sociological trends.

The group of undisguised idealists says outright that no historical laws exist, that history is an unknowable realm of chaos and chance.

Proponents of the *psychological* school see the basis of social development in psychological factors—the wishes, will and instincts of man. In their opinion, the cause of social disorder and the suffering of the working people in capitalist society is rooted in the imperfection of the worker's mentality and not in the objective laws of capitalism, not in private capitalist ownership. Perfection of mentality is the remedy offered by psychosociologists for curing major social ills.

The *biological* school favours scientific sociology in words, but in fact substitutes biological laws for the genuine laws of social development and places man on a level with animals blindly fighting for existence. This is an attempt to "justify", by allegedly natural laws, exploitation, predatory wars, colonialism, racialism and other ugly features of capitalism.

Bio-sociologists refuse to concede that it is scientifically untenable to reduce the laws of social development to biological laws because society develops according to its own specific laws, which qualitatively differ from the laws of development of animals and plants.

Rejection of the major laws of social development is also typical of *micro-sociology,* or, as it is also called, *empirical sociology.* Micro-sociologists do not openly reject knowledge of social life, but in the intricate chain of social phenomena they study only petty facts of capitalist reality, do not examine them in their interconnection, not wishing to see behind them the internal laws of society's development. This, in effect, signifies renunciation of consistent scientific analysis and the need to raise and solve the basic social problems of our time.

Refusal to recognise the laws of social development is nothing but an attempt to clear the way in social life for religious faith. There is nothing accidental in the fact that many bourgeois sociologists maintain that the historical process is predestined by God. For example, the English historian Arnold Toynbee insists that the aim of history is to set up the kingdom of God and history is God revealing himself.

By rejecting the law-governed character of social development, many bourgeois ideologists thereby distort the real course of history, embellish capitalism and attempt to justify its reactionary domestic and foreign policies.

Negation of Social Progress

The unscientific nature of contemporary bourgeois sociology is also manifested in the negation of historical progress and society's advance.

In this connection it should be noted that the views of sociologists on the character of the historical process have undergone important changes. When the emerging capitalist class was fighting for power, bourgeois enlighteners had a lot to say about social progress. The idea of progress served the bourgeoisie as a weapon for breaking up the old feudal system and establishing the more progressive capitalist society. But once the capitalist class came to power its understanding of social progress became amazingly one-sided. The ideologists of the bourgeoisie began to praise the capitalist order to the skies and to hold it up as the eternal kingdom of freedom and justice, an embodiment of the ideals of progress. Bourgeois sociologists declare that the aim of social progress has been attained and that there is no further road ahead. It is fear of the future which holds out no favourable prospect for capitalism, and fear of the new, communist world that is logically coming to replace the old bourgeois society, that makes them negate progress.

Quite often contemporary bourgeois sociologists put up in contrast to the concepts of "progress" and "development" the term "social change" which they apply to numerous secondary processes that take place in society and exert no noticeable influence on the course of history, and thus side-step the question of the progressive nature of social development. They want thereby to divert attention from the radical, revolutionary changes now taking place in society, to belittle their significance, and also to avoid solving the burning social problems of our age.

Renunciation of the idea of social progress by bourgeois sociologists is also manifested in the numerous theories of the "cycle", "stagnation" and "regress" of society which they are now assiduously spreading.

In the 1920s, the "cycle" theory was preached by the ideologist of German imperialism, Oswald Spengler. In his book *The Decline of the West* he sought to prove that society is unable to escape the "vicious circle" in which the selfsame three stages are invariably repeated: rise, apex and decline. In Spengler's opinion, capitalism is the apex of civilisation and culture. With its decline mankind will inevitably revert to barbarism. From this follows condemnation of the fight against capitalism and rejection of the need for the socialist revolution and socialism, which are alleged to be generally impossible since society cannot arrive at something new.

In recent years the reactionary theory of the "historical cycle" has been revived by Arnold Toynbee who negates the universal progressive development of society, calling it an "illusion of progress". By opposing socialism and asserting that all attempts to undermine capitalism lead to the degeneration and decline of civilisation, Toynbee endeavours to present capitalist society as eternal and inviolable.

Life Overturns the Views of Bourgeois Sociologists

Contemporary bourgeois ideologists misrepresent the course of historical process. Sensing the approaching collapse of capitalism, they shout about the death of civilisation and humanity in general, and identify the inevitable doom of capitalism with the doom of humanity. Capitalism will definitely perish, but humanity will continue to live and develop and will certainly rise to the shining peaks of communism.

Bourgeois sociologists misrepresent the character of the historical process for a definite reason: to stave off the doom of capitalism, embellish the crumbling facade of the capitalist edifice, and vilify socialism and refute Marxism-Leninism, the sole scientific teaching of society.

To attain these objectives the enemies of Marxism slander socialism and Marxist-Leninist theory, justify capitalism and deliver false discourses about a "people's state", about a bourgeois state being a "welfare state". They evolved the notorious theory of convergence which claims that since advanced capitalist and socialist countries have highly developed industry, technology, science and other common features, the world is witnessing the drawing together of capitalism and socialism and their transformation into a sort of a synthetic society based, of course, on slightly modernised capitalism. Sometimes this synthetic society is called "single industrialised society" and lately either a "post-industrial" or "technotronic" society which derives its essence wholly from an exceptionally high level of scientific and technical development. It goes without saying, of course, that a convergence of these two opposing social systems is inconceivable, if only because capitalism rests on private ownership and exploitation, while socialism rests on public ownership and on relations of cooperation and mutual assistance of the working people.

However hard the apologists of imperialism try, history follows its course and most forcefully demonstrates the great truth of Marxism-Leninism.

Science and the history-making activity of the people prove beyond all doubt that social progress is a continuous natural historic process which takes place in keeping with objective laws that are independent of man. The history of society is an endless chain of development, revolutionary transitions from the more simple, lower social systems to the more complex, higher ones. Moreover, social progress is based on the growth and improvement of material production. In its development production has moved from principal tools—sticks and stones—with which man began his battle for survival, to sophisticated automatic machines and mechanisms driven by electric and atomic energy. As production advances, so do other spheres of social life.

Life, the enormous economic, social and cultural progress in the USSR and other socialist countries, humanity's advance from capitalism to socialism shatter the pseudo-scientific theories of contemporary bourgeois sociologists. All these "theories" strikingly evidence the crisis that has gripped modern capitalism and the reactionary sociology that defends it.

CHAPTER II

A Socio-economic Formation

The cornerstone of historical materialism is the teaching about socio-economic formation which is based on a historically determined mode of production of material wealth. But production can only take place if there are definite natural requisites: a geographical environment and population. Let us examine these requisites and ascertain their importance in social life.

1. Natural Requisites for the Life of Society

Geographical Environment and Society

Society as a distinct entity is a part of nature. It is inseparable from the rest of nature and constantly interacts with it. That part of nature, with which society interacts most closely and influences and is in turn influenced by, is called *geographical environment,* and includes climate, soil, rivers and seas, vegetable and animal life, relief and minerals.

The geographical environment is a *necessary condition* for man's productive activity. Without interaction with nature no labour, no productive activity is conceivable. In the struggle against nature man gains his means of subsistence.

The geographical environment can exert a dual influence on the development of society. Favourable natural conditions (mineral resources, forest, rivers, a good climate, etc.) promote society's development. On the other hand, unfavourable natural conditions adversely affect social development. The absence of minerals, for example, impedes industrial development; an arid climate hinders the progress of agriculture, etc.

Acting on the importance of the geographical environment in social development, proponents of the *geographical trend* in sociology overestimate its role and claim that social development is determined either by the environment as a whole or by some of its elements—the climate, rivers, etc.

It is clear that the geographical trend is scientifically untenable. It does not and cannot explain the causes of social development, or why, for instance, two countries which are developing in approximately the same

12

geographical conditions stand at different levels of economic and political organisation.

The geographical trend does not take into account that, while being subject to the influence of nature, society on its part actively acts upon nature, and that as it transforms and makes nature serve its interests, society accelerates and modifies certain natural processes. The extent to which society acts upon the geographical environment in the final analysis depends on the level of development of production, science and technology. The socialist system, where society for the first time in history can consciously and in a planned way transform nature in the interests of the working man, creates particularly favourable conditions for acting upon nature.

It follows that the geographical environment is not the determining factor in society's development, although it is a necessary condition of social life. It is only capable of facilitating or retarding society's development.

*Noosphere**

Human society and the natural environment are organically interlinked. This interaction results in "humanised nature" which Vernadsky called the *noosphere*. "The biosphere," he wrote, "has passed, or, to be more exact, is passing into a new evolutionary condition, the noosphere, and is being assimilated through the scientific thought of social humanity."** Vernadsky was the first to describe the evolution of the planet Earth as a single cosmic, geological, biogenic and anthropogenic process and demonstrated the enormous transforming effect of human thought and science and its increasing effect on the natural environment, an effect which has acquired a truly global scale. While noting the ever greater independence of the power of reason of the environment and of various natural conditions, he called for the conservation and maintenance of the balance that exists in nature and the biosphere.

The noosphere appeared with the emergence of mankind, which by developing and constantly improving technology has enormously affected the natural environment on the Earth and terrestrial space. The noosphere is an enormous component of the universe which is continuously growing as man's influence on nature extends and deepens. Its specific characteristics are social involvement and dependence on a social form of movement.

---

* Derived from the Greek word *noo* meaning "mind."
** V.I. Vernadsky, *The Naturalist's Reflections. The Scientific Thought as a Planetary Phenomenon*, Book 2, Moscow, 1977, p. 21 (in Russian).

The very term noosphere implies the need for a reasoned, scientific approach to the interaction between society and nature, an approach which is incompatible with a purely consumer, let alone commercial attitude to it.

The noosphere is a unity, an interaction of nature and society, with the latter being primary since rational human activity is the dominating factor. Society leaves its mark on the environment and influences and transforms it through the power of the human brain and the human hand. It is characteristic that many of the material components of society, such as the means of production and objects of consumption, are, in the final analysis, components of the environment that have been transformed by man and that have acquired a social importance as a result of man's activity—the quality of being an object of ownership and a subject of the satisfaction of social and personal needs. In the process of transforming the environment, society assimilates, transforms the ever new elements of environment according to its interests and needs and turns the latter into its own components.

The natural part of the noosphere does not include the whole of nature, but only that part which has been *mastered by society* and which, to one degree or another, experiences the effects of the latter, being either assimilated, neutralised or rejected by it.

The features of the natural environment which are also components of the noosphere include abiotic elements (inorganic nature), biotic elements (flora and fauna) and cosmic elements which largely include terrestrial space that has been entered by man and which, in one way or another, serves his needs. In recent years, of course, the cosmic elements of the noosphere have been vastly extended so that studies are now being carried out not only on terrestrial space, but on the space around other planets of the solar system like the Moon. The noosphere is now extending its cosmic borders.

Population and Society

Population is another necessary condition for the material life of society. Production is impossible without people, whose labour constitutes the mighty force which subjugates nature and puts it to the service of man. In certain conditions, therefore, a large or small population and its high or low growth rate can accelerate or slow down a country's development. Large manpower resources and a high population growth rate are undoubtedly an important factor in the Soviet Union's great successes.

But does population play a decisive role in society's development? History answers this question in the negative. There are countries with a high population density and growth rate which lag economically, politically and culturally behind countries with considerably lower population density and slower growth rates.

This means that population density and growth do not determine society's progress. On the contrary, they themselves depend on the character of a social system

Nevertheless, supporters of *malthusianism,* a reactionary trend in bourgeois sociology, proceed from the assumption that it is the growth of population that determines the course of social development. The father of this theory, the English clergyman and economist Thomas Malthus, at the end of the 18th century announced his "discovery" of the "universal principle" that the means of subsistence grow in arithmetical progression, while the population grows in geometrical progression and that this is the cause of the poverty, starvation, unemployment and other suffering which afflict the working people. Malthus also proposed a "way" to get rid of these evils—the poor should abstain from marrying and having children.

Malthus needed the pseudo-scientific "theory" of population to exonerate capitalism and to justify the hardships capitalism inflicts on the working people. Malthusianism is now used by the imperialist bourgeoisie to mask the deep contradictions of imperialism, and to justify their aggressive foreign policy. Present-day malthusianism has become openly misanthropic: it no longer confines itself to preaching celibacy and birth control, but proposes that H-bombs, germ warfare and other monstrous means of destruction should be used to do away with the "superfluous" mouths.

Science and practical experience refute malthusianism. Marx proved that the causes of the working people's poverty and starvation under capitalism are rooted not in the natural laws of population, but in the very essence of the capitalist system, in the extremely unjust distribution of material wealth. The lion's share of this wealth is appropriated by the capitalists, while the working people are often deprived of even the most essential means of subsistence. Malthusianism has been conclusively refuted by the economic progress of the Soviet Union and other socialist countries where capitalism has been abolished, and starvation, poverty and unemployment have been banished for all time, where man's life is becoming increasingly secure and prosperous.

Neither the geographical environment nor the population are the determining factors in social development. The determining factor is the mode of production of material wealth, which we shall now examine.

2. Mode of Production—the Determinative Force of Social Development

People cannot exist without food, clothing, shelter and other necessities of life. Nature, however, does not provide these things ready-made; to produce them people must work. Labour is, therefore, the basis of social life, a natural necessity for man. Without labour, without productive activity, human life itself would be impossible. *The production of material wealth* is consequently the chief, determinative factor of social development.

Productive Forces

In the labour process people transform natural objects to satisfy their needs. To make a machine, for example, iron ore is mined, smelted, converted into steel and then treated accordingly.

Material production is impossible without the objects and means of labour.

Objects of labour are the things to which human labour is applied. *Means of labour* are the machines, equipment, tools, production buildings, transport and so on. The objects and means of labour constitute the *means of production.*

Instruments of production, with which people act on objects of labour and transform them, are the most important means of labour. Production is inconceivable without instruments of labour, as nature does not willingly part with its riches and they cannot be wrested by brawn alone. Man can only gain his means of livelinood with the aid of these instruments and the better they are, the greater means of livelihood he gets.

Instruments of labour on their own, however, do not produce material wealth. They must not only be made, but also be put to use. The most perfect machine will eventually turn into a useless pile of metal if no human hand touches it. Only man can set a tool in motion and organise material production. That is why he is an essential element of production.

The productive forces are the means of production, and above all the instruments of labour created by society and the people who produce the material wealth. In our age of the great scientific and technical revolution, science, as we shall see further on, is increasingly turning into a direct productive force.

The productive forces determine the relations of man to nature and his power over it. *The working people* are the principal element of the productive forces. People's constructive labour sets in motion the tools they have devised and makes these implements give mankind the immeasurable quantities of the things it needs.

Relations of Production

Productive forces are not the only factors in material production. People can only produce jointly by organising in a society. That is why labour is and always has been social in character. "In order to produce," Marx wrote, "they [people—*V.A.*] enter into definite connections and relations with one another and only within these social connections and relations does their action with nature, does production take place."*

People were connected by labour at the dawn of primitive society. In nomad hunting tribes, for example, this connection was that of fellow-hunters. As the productive forces and the division of labour grew, the relations between people became more and more diverse. Connections were established between crop growers and herdsmen, peasants and craftsmen, craftsmen and merchants, etc. With the development of the machine industry, the connections between the producers became especially diverse and manysided.

People's relations in the production process constitute *relations of production,* which are an integral part of material production. A certain historical *mode of production* therefore, appears as the *unbreakable* unity between the productive forces and the corresponding relations of production.

Relations of production are based on the *form of ownership,* i.e., the relation of people to the means of production—the land, its mineral resources, forests, waters, raw materials, factory buildings, instruments of labour and so on. On the form of ownership depends the dominating or subordinate *position of various social groups in production,* their relations in the production process or, as Marx put it, the mutual exchange of their activity. If property is publicly owned (if the means of production belong to the working people), relations of production assume the nature of cooperation and mutual assistance between workers free of exploitation, as is the case under socialism. If property is privately owned (if the means of production belong to the exploiting minority) the relations of production are relations of domination, subordination and exploitation characteristic, for example, of capitalism. Since the working people in an antagonistic class society are deprived of the means of production they are forced to work for the exploiters who own these means.

The *form of distribution* also depends on the nature of the ownership of the means of production. Private capitalist ownership determines the

* Karl Marx, "Wage Labour and Capital", in: Karl Marx, Frederick Engels, *Collected Works,* Vol. 9, Moscow, 1977, p. 211.

extremely unjust distribution of society's material wealth under capitalism. The owner of the means of production appropriates most of the wealth produced, although he himself does not take a direct part in production. Public ownership in socialist society ensures the principle of distribution according to work, which meets the interests of all the working people. Under socialism all the material wealth produced belongs to the people.

The sphere of production relations encompasses the forms of ownership of the means of production and also the consequent position of the various social groups in production and the forms of distribution of material wealth.

Relations of production are formed *objectively,* independent of people's will and desire, on the basis of the development of the productive forces.

The mode of production develops by virtue of its own causes, its intrinsic dialectics. Let us examine these causes, and the internal dialectics of the development of production.

Dialectics of the Productive Forces and Relations of Production

Production does not stand still, it constantly grows, develops and improves. It could not be otherwise, for in order to live people must produce material wealth, and produce it on a growing scale. This is necessary because the number of people on our planet is continuously growing and their requirements are increasing all the time. Primitive man needed very little: coarse food, an animal skin, a cave or a roof over his head and a fire in his hearth. But the material and cultural needs of the person today are very, very great.

The only way to satisfy the increasing needs of the ever growing number of people is to constantly expand and improve production. *Development of production is an objective necessity, a law of social life.* The history of society is the law-governed development of social production, the necessary process of replacing a lower mode of production by another, higher one.

How does production develop?

The development of production begins with a change in the productive forces. But the productive forces, as we have learned, are instruments of production and the people who utilise these instruments. Which of these elements of the productive forces develops first? History shows that within the framework of the productive forces the instruments of production develop first. To lighten labour, to obtain more material wealth with the least expenditure of labour people constantly improve the existing instruments and devise new and more efficient ones.

The development and improvement of the instruments of production, technical progress, are a result of the work of the people engaged in production. But together with improvement of the instruments of labour, people themselves develop. Their production know-how and skill grow and new trades emerge. In the long run, as the instruments of labour improve and the workers develop, the relationship of people in the production process, the relations of production, also change.

The productive forces give rise to and form definite relations of production. But the productive forces existing at a certain time bring into being only those production relations which correspond to the internal nature of these forces. The capitalist manufacture which originated within feudalism brought into being capitalist, and no other, relations of production.

Arising on the basis of the productive forces, the relations of production themselves, too, do not remain passive. They *actively influence* the productive forces, accelerating or retarding their development. We should bear in mind that progressive, new production relations, corresponding to the nature of the productive forces, *accelerate* the development of social production and are the prime mover in the development of tne productive forces. On the other hand, old production relations wnich lag behind the development of the productive forces *hinder* their advance.

Production relations must conform to the nature of the productive forces for production to develop. In one form or another this has been the case in all the socio-economic formations. In the pre-socialist formations based on private property and exploitation, however, production relations cannot permanently conform to the developing productive forces. It is only at the initial stage of such mode of production that production relations conform to the nature of the productive forces and consequently act as the prime mover in the development of production. Then the production relations gradually became obsolete, lag behind the development of the productive forces, and this results in a contradiction between the new productive forces and the old production relations.

This contradiction is not accidental, it stems from the intrinsic nature of various sides of social production. Productive forces are the most mobile element of production. They constantly change, and even within the bounds of the same mode of production these changes can be very considerable. As regards the relations of production, they, too, undergo certain changes, but basically remain unaltered within the bounds of the given mode of production. During the existence of capitalism, for example, its productive forces have undergone deep changes, but the relations of production today, as before, are based on private capitalist ownership.

Being more stable, production relations do not keep pace with the development of the productive forces and, falling behind, begin to retard their advance and come into contradiction with them. As the productive forces develop further, the retarding role of the production relations is felt more and more, and the contradiction between the two becomes more acute, growing ultimately into a conflict. Social revolution becomes a necessity in order to destroy the old production relations and introduce new ones.

This is the objective dialectics of the productive forces and relations of production in an antagonistic class society.

3. The Interaction of the Economic Basis and the Superstructure of Society

We have already stated that the mode of production of material wealth is the chief, determinative force of social development. *How* the mode of production and the relations of production shape all the other social relations (political, legal, moral, etc.) and how the latter, in their turn, influence society's economic development are questions answered by the Marxist-Leninist theory of basis and superstructure.

What Is the Basis and the Superstructure?

Of all the diverse social relations, historical materialism singles out the *material, production relations* as the main and determinative ones. It is the totality of these production relations that constitutes the economic structure of society, its *basis*. The totality of production relations should be understood to mean the forms of property and, arising out of them, the relations between people in the process of production and the way material wealth is distributed.

Each society has its own basis. The type of basis as the totality of production relations depends on the condition of the productive forces. No basis can appear until the corresponding material conditions, the productive forces necessary for its birth, arise within the old society.

Once it arises, the basis plays a tremendous part in the life of society. It enables people to organise the production and distribution of material wealth. Without entering into economic relations, people cannot produce and consequently, cannot distribute the means of subsistence.

The basis is important because it serves as the *real foundation* upon which the *superstructure* arises, i. e., political, legal, philosophical, moral, artistic and religious views and their corresponding relations, institutions and organisations. That is why the basis is that aspect of the mode of production which *directly* moulds the *face* of society, its ideas and institutions.

The superstructure also plays a very important role in social development. Arising on a definite economic basis, it ultimately expresses the attitude of people to this basis. Various ideas help people to justify the need to strengthen or destroy the given basis, while institutions and organisations (the state, political parties, etc.) enable them to apply these ideas. It is through the basis that the superstructure influences the development of the productive forces.

Determinant Role of the Basis in Relation to the Superstructure

The superstructure *is brought into being* by the basis and is inseparably bound up with it. The superstructure depends on the basis. Let us take, for example, the basis of primitive society. The absence of private property and classes, and consequently of class contradictions, was the reason why the superstructure of primitive society had neither state, political and legal ideas, nor the corresponding institutions.

The birth of private property and classes, i. e., the appearance of the basis of slave-owning society, brought into being a superstructure of a different kind. Ideas were conceived which justified the rule of the slave-owner over the slave and also institutions (the state and others) protecting this rule.

The basis of an antagonistic class society has its contradictions. By expressing the different relationships of people to the means of production, it reflects the antithesis of class interests, the antagonism between the oppressed and the oppressors. The economic basis of modern capitalism, for example, is marked above all by antagonism between the bourgeoisie and the proletariat, although the economic structure of bourgeois society must not be confined only to the relationship between these two main antagonistic classes. In addition to the bourgeoisie and the proletariat capitalist society has other classes and social groups—the working peasants, artisans and the petty bourgeoisie in both town and country, whose interests clash with those of the monopoly bourgeoisie.

Since it is a reflection of the contradictions in the basis, the superstructure of an antagonistic class society also contains contradictions. It includes the ideas and institutions of different classes and social groups, but the ideas and institutions of the class that dominates economically prevail. "...The class, which is the ruling *material* force of society, is at the same time its ruling *intellectual* force,"* wrote Marx and Engels. Under capitalism the bourgeoisie dominates economically so that bourgeois ideas and institutions prevail and are used by the bourgeoisie to fight the working class and to perpetuate its own rule.

In capitalist society the bourgeoisie, however, is opposed by the working class which forms its own ideas and sets up its own institutions. Gradually the proletarians begin to understand the essence of capitalism and become aware of the need to abolish it. They set up their own organisations to fight the bourgeoisie—a political party, trade unions, co-operatives, and so on. In the course of the revolutionary struggle the working class masters Marxist theory creates its own morality, and its own political, legal and aesthetic views.

The determinative role of the basis in relation to the superstructure is manifested not only in the basis giving rise to the superstructure, but also in that the essential changes in the economic system necessarily lead to changes in the superstructure. During the transition from pre-monopoly capitalism to imperialism, for example, the capitalist economy underwent important change: free competition gave way to monopoly. The bourgeois superstructure also changed accordingly. In a number of countries the capitalist class went over or is going over from bourgeois-democratic forms of government to reactionary—fascist or semi-fascist forms. The rights of the working people are being increasingly curtailed and Communist parties and progressive organisations are not infrequently being persecuted. Bourgeois art and morality are degenerating, reactionary forms of idealism are becoming predominant in philosophy.

The changes in the superstructure are especially deep when one economic basis supersedes another as a result of social revolution. In the course of a revolution the political rule of the old class is replaced by the rule of the new class. A new state machinery (the system of political and legal institutions) is created in place of the old one. Social consciousness changes: the old ideology is ousted by the new corresponding to the new basis. "The old 'superstructure' falls apart," Lenin wrote, "and... a new one is created by the independent action of the most diverse social forces."*

* Karl Marx and Frederick Engels, "The German Ideology", in: Karl Marx, Frederick Engels, *Collected Works,* Vol. 5, p. 59.
* V. I. Lenin, "Revolution Teaches," *Collected Works,* Vol. 9, p. 146.

Relative Independence
and Active Role of the Superstructure

The superstructure, brought into being by the basis, also possesses *relative independence* which is manifested in the *continuity* of its development. A revolution in the superstructure, which takes place when the old basis is replaced by the new, does not signify the automatic elimination of all the features of the old superstructure. With the destruction of the old basis, the old superstructure as a whole, as a system of views and institutions of the old society, ceases to exist. But its individual features outlive the basis which gave rise to the old superstructure and pass into the superstructure of the new society. The new superstructure takes only those elements from the old one that can serve the classes of the new society, and are consistent with their interests. For instance, a newly emerged exploiter society assimilates only those ideas of the old superstructure which vindicate exploitation and uphold political and legal institutions of the exploiters.

The superstructure of any society also has non-transitory features which are important for all mankind. These include man's general moral standards and the finest creations of literature and art.

Because of its continuity, the superstructure of each society is very complex. It incorporates both the ideas and institutions inherited from the old society and the ideas and institutions which grew up on its current economic basis.

The relative independence of the superstructure is also seen in that, having arisen on the economic basis, it plays an *active part* in the development of this basis. The ideas and institutions prevailing in an antagonistic class society protect and strengthen its basis. They justify the rule of the class which brought them into being and whose interests they are destined to defend. In antagonistic societies these ideas and institutions are the theoretical means of sanctifying and organising the struggle of the ruling class against other classes, above all against the working classes, stifling their desire for liberation from exploitation, colonial and other oppression.

Let us take, for example, bourgeois ideas and institutions. When the capitalist basis was taking root, they actively contributed to its development and consolidation and were a powerful weapon in the struggle against the feudal class. Now that the capitalist basis has been doomed by history, bourgeois ideas and institutions are used for crushing progressive forces in order to preserve it at any cost, and to prevent or at least postpone the fall of capitalism. Capitalism is still alive, above all, because its interests are guarded by the bourgeois state and law, by all the media of ideological influence which play an extremely big role in the defence of capitalism.

4. Socio-Economic formation—a Complex Social Organism

Now that we have studied the mode of production of material wealth, the economic basis and the superstructure of society, we can extend and deepen our ideas of the socio-economic formation and realise that it is a complex social organism. The mode of production is the material and economic basis of a formation, its backbone, or shall we say, its skeletal frame, while its economic and spiritual image is characterised by the superstructure. Consequently, production, basis and superstructure are the key links, the components of any socio-economic formation, but with distinctive features in each given formation.

Besides production, basis and superstructure a socioeconomic formation is characterised by other social features: specific historical human communities (tribe, clan, nationality, nation), mode of life, family and marriage, language, natural sciences and certain public organisations (scientific and technical, and sports). Without being parts either of the basis or of the superstructure, these features are essential components of any formation, for without them society cannot exist and develop. Indeed, can people work and think without language which is a means of intercourse and exchange of views, or to reproduce the human race without family and marriage? Of course they cannot.

As a rule, all these features are typical of all formations and are subject to profound change in the course of transition from one formation to another. The forms of human communities change: in the primitive society the typical human communities were clans and tribes, under feudalism there were nationalities, and under capitalism—nations. With the transition from capitalism to socialism bourgeois nations are replaced by socialist nations. The mode of life, family and marriage, etc., change with each successive formation. As regards language, it changes in the process of social development and can pass from one formation to another. This also applies to achievements in natural science which are also assimilated and used in everyday life and in the process of labour by people in different formations.

The social phenomena comprising a socio-economic formation are *organically connected* and influence each other either directly or indirectly so that a formation is a *complex, developing social organism.*

We have already spoken about the unity and direct interaction of the productive forces and production relations, the basis and the superstructure. The superstructure is also connected with the productive forces, though not directly but through the economic basis. Elements of the superstructure also interact: politics, for example, influences art, morality, philosophy and other forms of the spiritual life of the people. Production, basis and superstructure leave their imprint on family relations, on the mode of life, etc. In a word, a socio-economic formation is wickerwork of the most diverse social phenomena whose interaction is occasioned above all by material production which permeates all the different social phenomena, determines the role and importance of each one of them, and dominates and transforms them in conformity with its own nature.

By showing the inviolable unity of social phenomena and their material basis, the concept of socio-economic formation completely overturns idealistic and metaphysical social theories which were predominant in pre-Marxist philosophy. The concept of formation also puts an end to the non-historical, abstract views of social life and shows that there is no such thing as society in general, but only a *concrete historical* society, i. e., a society which, to quote Marx, stands "at a *definite stage of historical development, a society with a peculiar distinctive character*".* Every society has its own, intrinsic productive forces, a certain type of production relations, a specific spiritual life, etc. In conformity with the general laws of history, every society also has its own, specific laws. The intrinsic laws of the communist formation, for example, are the law of planned, proportionate development of the national economy, the law of satisfying the growing requirements of people, the law of uninterrupted crisis-free development of the productive forces, etc.

Thus, the concept of socio-economic formation makes it possible to sort out all the historical formations and events. And although none of them are exact replicas of others, the concept of socio-economic formation enables us to single out what is most *essential, common* and *recurrent,* i. e., to disclose the laws of social development. This means that history is not a haphazard, chaotic conglomeration of phenomena, but a *law-governed natural historic process* of replacement of one socio-economic formation by another, higher and better one. At the same time the objective basis of what is common and recurrent—a historically definite type of production relations corresponding to a no less definite nature of production relations—is brought to light. "...Only the reduction of social relations to production relations and of the latter to the level of the productive forces, provided a firm basis for the conception that the development of formations of society is a process of natural history."**

---

* Karl Marx, "Wage Labour and Capital", in: Karl Marx, Frederick Engels, *Collected Works,* Vol. 9, p. 212.
** V. I. Lenin, "What the 'Friends of the People' Are and How They Fight the Social-Democrats", *Collected Works,* Vol. 1, pp. 140-141.

The elaboration of the teaching about socio-economic formations has made it possible to *periodise history on a strictly scientific basis*. The primitive-communal, slave-owning, feudal, capitalist and communist formations are the most important stages, or periods of history, whose succession was law-governed and a natural historical necessity. Neither does history stand still within the framework of each socio-economic formation. Historical development is not only a series of qualitative changes, of gigantic leaps from formation to formation; it also moves from a lower to a higher phase within one and the same formation. Capitalism goes through two stages of development—pre-monopoly and monopoly, or imperialist. The communist formation also develops from the lower stage—socialism, to the higher—mature communism.

History also shows that not all nations necessarily pass through all the formations without exception in their development. Slav and German tribes moved from the tribal system directly to feudalism, bypassing the slave-owning system. Some peoples (in the Central Asian republics of the USSR, and in the Mongolian People's Republic) attained socialism bypassing not only capitalism, but also partially the stage of mature feudalism. But this does not refute the *general objective tendency* of mankind's development from one formation to another, nor does it violate the *unity of the entire historical process*.

The fact that the concept of socio-economic formation discloses that which is common and recurrent in the development of peoples in various countries and continents does not mean that peoples in one and the same formation have no specific features of their own. These features, for example, manifest themselves in the *uneven rates* and *varying levels* of their development. This is due to the fact that in different countries elements of one or another formation do not mature at one and the same time, to specific internal and external factors, but chiefly to the nature and the essence of the formation itself. For instance, in capitalist society, particularly when it is in the imperialist stage, the law of the uneven economic and political development of different countries comes into operation. The transition to socialism is accompanied by the gradual approximation of levels of economic development, and when communism triumphs on Earth there will no longer be differences in the rates and levels of development.

Thus, a socio-economic formation, from the point of view of the countries concerned, presents a very complex and varied picture. Moreover, history knows no absolutely "pure" formations. In every formation there are survivals of the past in various spheres of social activity, and also the embryos or requisites of the new formation. Large-scale capitalist production, for example, is the material prerequisite of socialism, and the working class which arose on the basis of this production is the social force whose mission is to establish socialism.

It follows that the development of society is a law-governed, natural historical process of humanity's movement from formation to formation. Moreover, being a tendency this movement forces its way through a mass of concrete and very diverse historical factors. Let us now investigate humanity's advance from formation to formation in greater detail.

5. The History of Society as the History of Development and Law-Governed Succession of Socio-Economic formations

History knows five succeeding socio-economic formations: primitive-communal, slave-owning, feudal, capitalist and communist. We shall examine them in this order.

Primitive Communal Formation

The history of society begins with the appearance of man whose ability to make and use implements of labour sets him apart from animals. Labour holds the most important place in the emergence and development of man. It was in the process of labour that man himself was moulded and the forms of his social organisation arose and developed.

The primitive-communal system was the first and lowest form of organisation of people and it existed for tens of thousands of years. During this long period man succeeded in advancing from the use of objects of nature—sticks and stones—to making primitive tools. At first these were crude adzes, knives, chisels, javelins and spears, fishing hooks, etc., made of stone, wood, horn or bone. As time went on these implements were improved and carefully shaped. Then new implements appeared—bows and arrows, boats, sleighs and so on. Man learned how to make fire, which was of particularly great importance for the progress of humanity.

Together with the perfection of implements, people developed and improved their work. From the gathering of natural products (edible fruit, berries and grasses) man went over to cultivating plants, to farming, and from hunting wild animals, to their taming and domestication, to livestock raising.

The extremely low level of the productive forces under the primitive-communal system also determined the corresponding relations of production, which were based on common ownership of the means of production and were therefore relations of cooperation and mutual assistance between people. These relations were conditioned by the fact that people with their primitive implements could only withstand the mighty forces of nature together, collectively.

In primitive society people lived in groups, in clans based on consanguineous ties. They worked the communal land together with common tools, had a common dwelling which sheltered them from bad weather and wild beasts. The products they obtained were shared equally. The level of the productive forces was so low that people barely managed to obtain enough food to survive. There was nothing that could be appropriated. Therefore, private property, classes and, consequently, exploitation did not exist.

Even in primitive society the productive forces developed steadily, though very slowly. The instruments of labour were improved and skills were gradually accumulated. The transition from stone to metal tools was a tremendous leap forward in production. The new implements—the wooden plough with a metal plough-share, the bronze or iron axe, etc.—made labour more productive. It became possible to grow crops and raise livestock on a wider scale. The first big social division of labour took place when stock raising became separated from crop growing. Later the crafts (making of tools, weapons, clothing, footwear, etc.) emerged as an independent branch of production. Exchange of products began to develop.

With the growth of labour productivity the clan began to break up into families. Private property arose and the family became the owner of the means of production. However, the means of production were mainly concentrated in the hands of families of the former clan elite. Since the producer began to make more things than were necessary for his own subsistence, the possibility arose of appropriating the surplus product and, consequently, of some members of society enriching themselves by exploiting others. The spread of private property and commodity exchange speeded up the disintegration of the clan. Primitive equality gave way to social inequality. The first antagonistic classes, slaves and slave-owners, appeared.

This is how the development of the productive forces led to the replacement of primitive society by slave-owning society.

Slave-Owning Formation

The productive forces inherited from primitive society were further developed in the *slave-owning socio-economic formation*. The wooden and stone implements were completely superseded at first by bronze and then iron implements. The wooden plough with a metal plough-share and then the iron plough, the metal sickle and other implements increased labour productivity in agriculture. Alongside crop growing the cultivation of fruit and vegetables arose. People built canals, dykes, water-raising devices, etc. to irrigate the land, and mills to mill grain into flour. Ore mining and smelting developed, with people employing the simplest tools such as picks and hammers for mining the ore, crushing mills or mortars for crushing the ore, and primitive furnaces for smelting the metal.

The division of labour continued. In the crafts various branches ermerged: metal smelting and forging, making of weapons, clothing and footwear, weaving, tanning, pottery making etc. More and more special tools were used by the craftsmen and a primitive lathe and bellows appeared.

Construction, shipbuilding and weapon-making became widely developed, towns grew up and commerce spread.

The development of the productive forces in the slaveowning formation was promoted by the corresponding production relations. These relations were based on the slave-owner's absolute ownership of both the means of production and the slave himself and everything he produced. The owner left the slave only the bare minimum necessary to keep him from dying of starvation.

Production relations, the economic basis of slave-ownership, gave rise to the social superstructure: the slave-owning state with diverse institutes of coercion (army, court, officialdom, etc.) and the ideology of the slave-owners. This superstructure faithfully served its basis and protected private property and exploitation.

In the slave-owning society there existed relations of domination and subjection, cruel exploitation by the handful of slave-owners of the mass of slaves who possessed no rights at all. For a time these relations promoted the development of the productive forces, but then their potentialities were exhausted and they became an impediment to the expansion of social production. Production demanded the constant improvement of implements, higher labour productivity, but the slave had no interest in this because it would not improve his position in the least. Moreover, the slave himself— the main productive force—owing to inhuman exploitation was both physically and mentally degraded.

As time went on the contradiction between the productive forces and the production relations in the slave-owning society became extremely acute. This contradiction was manifested in slave revolts. The slaves, ruthlessly exploited and brought to sheer desperation, rose up against their enslavers. These revolts, together with raids from neighbouring tribes, undermined the foundations of the slave-owning system, and on its ruins arose a new, *feudal formation.*

Feudal formation

The progressive development of the productive forces continued under *feudalism.* It was in this period that men began to employ, in addition to their muscular strength, the power of water and wind, to make use of water- and winddriven mills, sailing ships, etc. Men learned how to produce iron out of pig iron, invented paper, gun-powder, book printing and made a number of other discoveries which played a great role in the history of mankind.

The crafts advanced further; new implements and machines were invented and old ones improved. Progress was particularly apparent in textile production in which a spinning-wheel, ribbon loom, twisting machine and other innovations were introduced. The labour of the craftsman became specialised, considerably raising productivity. With the development of the crafts and trade towns grew, some of them becoming major world craft and trading centres.

Agriculture made progress as new varieties of grain, fruit and vegetables were cultivated; the soil was tilled more thoroughly and fertilisers were introduced. Animal husbandry was extended, draught animals were employed on a wider scale and the output of animal products was increased.

The development of the productive forces under feudalism was facilitated by the feudal relations of production. These relations were based on the feudal lord's ownership of the means of production (mainly the land) and incomplete ownership of the serfs. The serfs had to work for the feudal lord and perform all kinds of labour services for him. He could buy and sell serfs, but their lives no longer belonged to him.

The production relations under feudalism, as in the slaveowning society, were relations of domination and subjection, exploitation of the serfs by the feudal lords. Nevertheless, they were more progressive, because they made the producer to some extent interested in his labour. The peasants and the artisans had their own property (the peasant could own a plot of land, a horse and other livestock, and farming implements; the artisan owned tools or simple machines) with which, after performing all feudal duties, they worked for themselves. They were interested in improving the implements and methods of farming and handicraft.

As regards feudal society's superstructure, it was in effect just as exploitative as that of the slave-owning formation. The only difference was that it protected the economic and political interests of the feudal lords and not of the slave-owners, and was designed to preserve and strengthen feudal private property and the production relations which rested on it, i.e., the economic basis of feudalism. The state apparatus and the armed forces expanded, religion became dominant in the intellectual life of society and was used by the ruling class to justify private property and the exploitation of the labouring people.

As time went on the productive forces continued to develop. A particularly big impetus to their progress was given by the great geographical discoveries at the turn of the 16th century (the discovery of America, the route to India, and so on). An international market began to take shape and the demand for various commodities increased, which handicraft production was no longer able to satisfy. Manufacture came to take the place of the handicraft workshop.

Manufacture brought together under one roof a large number of workers, introduced a wide division of labour between them and thereby greatly increased labour productivity. The rise of manufacture signified the birth within feudal society of new, capitalist production and its intrinsic, opposing classes—the bourgeoisie and the proletariat.

With the appearance of manufacture, the productive forces came into contradiction with the feudal production relations. Manufacture demanded a free worker while feudalism tied the serf to the land; manufacture needed a broad international market, the establishment of which was hampered by the closed feudal economy, its isolation and the natural economy. It became necessary to replace the feudal relations of production with new, capitalist relations. This was accomplished by a number of bourgeois revolutions in which the main fighting force were the serfs and the lower sections of the urban population led by the bourgeoisie.

Capitalist Formation

Large-scale machine production is the specific feature of the productive forces of *capitalism*. Huge factories, plants and mines took the place of artisan workshops and manufactures. "Subjection of Nature's forces to man, machinery, application of chemistry to industry and agriculture, steam-navigation, railways, electric telegraphs, clearing of whole continents for cultivation, canalisation of rivers, whole populations conjured out of the ground"*—this is how Marx and Engels described the capitalist pro-

* Karl Marx and Frederick Engels, "Manifesto of the Communist Party", in: Karl Marx, Frederick Engels, *Collected Works*, Vol. 6, p. 489.

ductive forces in the *Manifesto of the Communist Party*. In a century or two capitalism accomplished much more in developing the productive forces than had been done in all the preceding eras of human history.

This vigorous growth of the productive forces was facilitated by the capitalist relations of production, based on private capitalist ownership which gradually but inexorably ousted feudal ownership. Under capitalism the producer, the proletariat, is legally free, being attached neither to the land nor to any particular factory. He is free in the sense that he can go to work for any capitalist, but he is not free from the bourgeois class as a whole. Possessing no means of a production, he is compelled to sell his labour power and thereby come under the yoke of exploitation.

The production relations and the economic basis of capitalism gave rise to a corresponding superstructure—bourgeois ideas and institutions. The growing resistance of the working class to capitalist oppression and also the reactionary domestic and foreign policy of the bourgeoisie led to a gigantic growth of the state machinery, particularly of the armed forces and other organs of coercion. Spiritual life (political and legal views, art, morality, philosophy) is permeated with the spirit of capitalist profit, violence and inhumanity. The mission of the capitalist superstructure is ideologically to substantiate the permanence and inviolability of capitalist ownership and exploitation. The ideology of the working class arises and develops alongside bourgeois ideas and in the struggle against them.

Capitalist relations of production brought into being capitalist profit which is a great stimulus to the development of production. It is in the drive for profit that the capitalist extends production, improves machinery and production methods in industry and agriculture. These relations, however, not only determined an unprecedented growth in production, but also gave rise to productive forces which placed the capitalist system as a whole on the brink of doom. Marx and Engels likened capital to a sorcerer, whose incantations brought into action forces so powerful that he was unable to control them.

With the titanic growth of the productive forces, capitalist relations of production cease to correspond to them, and fetter their development. The deepest contradiction of the capitalist mode of production is the contradiction between the social character of production and the private capitalist form of appropriation. Production in capitalist society bears a strikingly pronounced social character. Many millions of workers are concentrated at large plants and take part in social production, while the fruits of their labour are appropriated by a small group of owners of the means of production. This is the basic economic contradiction of capitalism.

Towards the end of the last century capitalism grew into *imperialism*, its highest and last stage. The main feature of imperialism is the domination of monopolies, which replaces free competition. Monopolies are large associations of capitalists who concentrate in their hands the production and marketing of the bulk of commodities. The aim of the monopolies is to extract the highest profits possible.

To this end the imperialists intensify the exploitation of the working people in their own country and in the colonies and dependent countries. Having divided up the world among themselves, the imperialists engage in a bitter struggle for its re-division.

Imperialism aggravates all the contradictions of capitalist society to the extreme, especially the contradiction between the social character of production and the private form of appropriation. This contradiction gives rise to economic crises and unemployment, causes fierce class battles between the bourgeoisie and the proletarlat and constitutes the economic basis for the socialist revolution. The victorious socialist revolution abolishes the capitalist production relations and ushers in the new, communist socio-economic formation.

6. Communist Socio-Economic formation

The communist socio-economic formation, as we have said earlier, passes through two stages (phases)—socialism and communism—in its development.

Socialism

Socialism is characterised by domination of public ownership of the means of production and absence of exploitation. Consequently, it cannot rise in the womb of capitalism, like the capitalist system arose in feudal society.

This does not mean, however, that socialism springs up from nothing. The prerequisites for socialism—large-scale machine production, a high degree of concentration and socialisation of labour, and a high level of science and technology—arise under capitalism. The social force destined to build socialism, namely the working class, which becomes steeled in the struggle against the bourgeoisie, organises its own party and masters scientific ideology, also forms in capitalist society.

But these prerequisites alone are by no means all that is necessary for the building of socialism. Socialism does away with private ownership of the means of production, for ever abolishes exploitation and all forms of social, national and racial oppression. For this to happen a *socialist revolution* and then *a period of transition from capitalism to socialism* are necessary. In this period the working class, which has taken power in its hands together with all the working people, consciously and in a planned way builds the new, socialist society. Nationalisation, cooperation of agriculture, industrialisation and cultural revolution—these are the main elements of Lenin's plan for socialist construction which has been successfully carried into life by the Soviet people under the guidance of the Communist party. They have built up socialist production, and the basis and superstructure of socialism.

The foundation of socialism as that of any other society, is the production of material wealth. Socialist production is a dialectical unity of the productive forces and relations of production. Socialist industry and agriculture, transport and communications, the construction industry, and also people working in these spheres of the national economy, are the *productive forces* of socialist society.

The technological foundation of the socialist economy consists of large-scale, constantly progressing machine industry, based on the wide use of electricity and chemistry as well as atomic energy in some branches, and extensive mechanisation and partial automation. Heavy industry is the cornerstone of the socialist economy, the source of its might and wealth.

The people—workers, collective farmers, technicians and engineers—are the principal element of the productive forces of socialism. In Soviet times they have accumulated vast production experience; they are successfully operating the most diverse and intricate machines, and ensuring steady technical progress and the constant growth of labour productivity.

Development of the productive forces—constant improvement of the means of production and professional skill—is a necessary requisite for the socialist economy's progress.

Socialist relations of production have arisen and are developing on the basis of socialism's productive forces. These relations are founded on *social socialist ownership* of the means of production. There are two forms of social property: *state property,* belonging to the whole people represented by the socialist state, and *co-operative collective-farm property,* i.e., the property of individual collective farms or co-operatives. Both forms of property are socialist in character and ensure the accomplishment of the tasks of socialism. State property is the dominant form in socialist society.

Socialist ownership determines the production relations of *fraternal cooperation and mutual assistance* between workers. The greatest advantage of socialist production relations and their fundamental distinction from production relations in antagonistic class societies is that they preclude all exploitation of man by man.

The socialist principle of distribution according to work has been applied on the basis of socialist ownership. "He who does not work, neither shall he eat."

Socialist society has done away for ever with the antagonistic contradiction between the social character of production and the private form of appropriation inherent in capitalism. In socialist society, *relations of production conform to the character of the productive forces.* Under socialism production bears a strikingly pronounced social character. Millions of people work at large industrial and agricultural enterprises. But in contrast to capitalism where the fruits of the labour of millions are appropriated by a small group of exploiters, in socialist society the fruits of labour belong to the producers, the working people themselves. The dominance of social ownership, which constitutes the basis of socialist production relations, also determines the social nature of distribution. *Four-fifths* of the Soviet Union's national income goes to satisfy the personal material and cultural requirements of the working people. The rest of the national income is used for expanding production, for defence purposes and for other social needs, i.e., it also belongs to the working people.

Since they conform to the productive forces, socialist relations of production afford great scope for their advance and are a powerful factor in the expansion of production. It is not the quest for profit, but the interest of all the working people in production's progress that is the driving force behind the development of the socialist economy.

The socialist relations of cooperation and mutual assistance are most clearly evident in *socialist emulation,* through which the working people, displaying mass labour heroism, eliminate shortcomings in their work, assist those who lag behind and make them advance to the level of the leading workers.

Socialist production relations also provide a powerful stimulus to economic progress in the form of *material interest* of the workers in the results of their labour. The better and more efficiently a worker, collective farmer or intellectual works, the greater is his remuneration. This also benefits society. Organic *combination of personal and social interests* in socialist society is an important factor in the development of production.

Thanks to the socialist relations of production, the Soviet people, led by the Communist Party, have transformed backward Russia into a country with powerful industry and agriculture.

Socialist production relations ensure rapid economic growth in all the socialist countries. It is important to note that socialist production developed at a considerably faster rate than production in capitalist countries.

Socialist production relations are the *economic basis of socialism*. The necessary condition for building up the economic basis of socialism is the establishment of the working-class state. Having concentrated all the basic means of production in its hands, the proletarian state organises the planned development of socialist relations of production in town and country.

As distinct from the basis, some of the elements of the future socialist superstructure appear in the preceding capitalist formation. The Marxist-Leninist theory, the party of the working class, trade unions, proletarian morality, literature and art come into being during the domination of the capitalist basis and then become the superstructure of the socialist society. Moreover, this superstructure includes the greatest achievements in science, culture and philosophy of the preceding epochs. Yet all these elements do not make up the socialist superstructure as a totality of ideas and institutions. As a whole it is built only after the socialist basis is formed.

The socialist ideology and its institutions—the socialist state, the Communist party, the trade unions, the Komsomol, cultural and educational, defence and other organisations—make up the *socialist superstructure*.

The progressive socialist basis also determines the nature of the socialist superstructure, its dynamic, revolutionary, transforming nature. Reflecting the actual course of history—mankind's advance from capitalism to communism—the socialist superstructure promotes this movement with every means and strengthens and develops the socialist basis.

The distinguishing features of the socialist society's superstructure are its unity, absence of antagonistic contradictions, all of which are due to the solidity of the socialist basis. Under socialism there are no classes which entertain and spread reactionary ideas and views, and the absolute majority of the working people are interested in the further development of socialist society. The are doing everything possible to strengthen the economic basis of socialism, and broaden and improve its superstructure.

The socialist superstructure expresses and protects the interests of the working people and enjoys their unremitting backing. Hence its dynamism and its enormous influence on the development of the basis and the entire progress of socialist society. This is due to the vast scale of the tasks of cultural and economic development in the USSR, the active participation of ever increasing masses in public life and the heightening role of ideological education.

Developed Socialism

"In the USSR," states the Constitution of the USSR, "a developed socialist society has been built. At this stage, when socialism is developing on its own foundations, the creative forces of the new system and the advantages of the socialist way of life are becoming increasingly evident, and the working people are more and more widely enjoying the fruits of their great revolutionary gains."*

The distinctive features of developed socialism in the *economic* field are mighty productive forces which are utilised according to a single plan, stable rates of growth of production and of labour productivity on the basis of the latest achievements in science and technology, and a steadily rising wellbeing of the people.

In the *political* field it is a genuinely democratic political system which ensures effective administration of public life, increasingly active participation of the working people in state affairs, combination of rights and freedoms enjoyed by the citizens with their duties and responsibilities to society.

In the *social* field—mature socialist social relations which developed on the basis of full domination of socialist ownership, the established socio-political and ideological unity of society, and the socialist way of life; a new historical community—the Soviet people—has taken shape in developed socialist society.

In the *intellectual* sphere—a high level of science, culture and education, and universal spread and affirmation of the scientific, Marxist-Leninist world outlook.

Developed socialism is a society of working people—patriots and internationalists—with a high level of organisation, moral integrity and civic duty; a society whose law of life is the concern of all people for the wellbeing of each individual; a society in which increasingly favourable conditions for the all-round development of the individual are being formed. The stage of developed socialism is an essential link in the chain of social transformations, a relatively long stage in society's movement from capitalism to communism.

Communism

"*Communism,*" in the words of the CPSU Programme, "*is a classless*

---

* *Constitution (Fundamental Law) of the Union of Soviet Socialist Republics*, Moscow, 1977, p. 13

*social system with one form of public ownership of the means of production and full social equality of all members of society; under it, the all-round development of people will be accompanied by the growth of the productive forces through continuous progress in science and technology; all the springs of co-operative wealth will flow more abundantly, and the great principle 'From each according to his ability, to each according to his needs' will be implemented. Communism is a highly organised society of free, socially conscious working people in which public self-government will be established, a society in which labour for the good of society will become the prime vital requirement of everyone, a necessity recognised by one and all and the ability of each person will be employed to the greatest benefit of the people."** *

Communism shall fulfil the historic mission of delivering all people from social inequality, from every form of oppression and exploitaltion, from the horrors of war, and shall bring Peace, Labour, Freedom, Equality, Brotherhood and Happiness to all people on earth.

The establishment of communism in the world will bring deep changes in all spheres of life—production, social relations, culture and the way of life, people's ideas and views. Communism will provide all members of society with conditions of life which most fully meet the innermost aspirations of man and conform to the loftiest human ideals.

Communist society will be distinguished above all by a very high level of continuously expanding production and an unprecedentedly high level of labour productivity resulting from rapid scientitic and technical progress. Communist society will attain the highest stage of planned economy and ensure the most purposive and rational use of material wealth and natural resources. People will be equipped with the best and mightiest technology, man's power over nature will be raised to tremendous heights, enabling him to control its spontaneous forces to a much greater extent and to employ them in his own interests. The aim of communist production will be to ensure continuous social progress, to give each member of society material and cultural necessities and comforts, satisfying his constantly growing requirements, interests and tastes.

While catering for diverse needs of the people, however, communism will not be a society of anarchy, idleness and indolence. Labour will be the chief source of its material and spiritual wealth. Under communism everyone will voluntarily work according to his ability, multiplying the wealth and reinforcing the might of society. The very nature of work will change.

---

* *Road to Communism*, Moscow, 1962, p. 509.

Labour will cease to be merely a means of subsistence and will turn into life's prime want, into genuine creative endeavour, into a source of joy and happiness.

Communism will put an end to the division of society into classes and social groups. Workers and peasants as classes will disappear as distinctions between town and country are eradicated in the social and economic spheres, in culture and way of life, and as the two forms of socialist property merge into one communist property. Manual workers will attain the cultural and technical level of intellectuals and hence there will be no intelligentsia as a separate social group under communism. Each member of society will engage in mental and manual labour, and mental and physical efforts in his work will be organically combined.

All members of communist society, by virtue of their equal relation to the means of production, will be in the same position, enjoy equal conditions of work and distribution and actively participate in administering society's affairs. Harmonious relations between the individual and society will become the rule because social and personal interests will be fully combined.

Human culture will soar to unprecedented heights. The culture of communist society, inheriting and developing all the best created by world culture, will represent a new, higher stage in mankind's cultural development. It will incorporate all the diversity and wealth of spiritual life, the lofty ideals and humanism of the new society. It will be a classless, internationalist culture of all mankind.

Under communism there will be a new man, who will combine spiritual wealth with moral purity and physical perfection, and who will have a high communist consciousness, industriousness, discipline and devotion to society's interests. The exceptional organisation and precision demanded of man by communist production will be ensured not by compulsion but by a profound sense of civic duty. Man's development will be comprehensive and harmonious; his abilities and talents will be given full rein and will blossom forth, his finest spiritual and physical qualities will be manifested to the full.

The building of communism will signify the attainment of the Communist Party's supreme goal of building a society on whose banner will be inscribed: "From each according to his ability, to each according to his needs." The Party's slogan "Everything for the sake of Man, for the benefit of Man" will be applied in full measure.

CHAPTER III

The People—the Decisive Force in Social

Development. Society and the Individual

We have stated earlier that society develops on the basis of its own laws, historical necessity. But social laws are always manifested through the conscious deeds and actions of people who make their owm history.

Of what importance are people in the historical process, and what is the role of the people and the individual in history?

Historical materialism proceeds from the premise that the people are the makers of history. Let us find out why it is that people make history and what part the individual plays in social development.

1. The people Are the Real Makers
of History, the Decisive force in Social Development

What Is the People

In order to explain the people's role as the makers of history we must first be clear about what we mean by the people.

The people is not something which is immutable, that stands outside of history and is fixed once and for all. Nor is it a grey, disorderly "mob", "the rabble", hostile to any civilisation and progress, as the ideologists of the exploiting classes claim.

The people above all are those who work; in an antagonistic class society they are the exploited. In slave society they were chiefly the slaves, and in feudal society they were the serfs and artisans. In capitalist society the people include the working class, the peasants, the working intellectuals and other groups which contribute to social progress.

In an antagonistic class society the people constitute the majority of the population, but not the entire population. In contemporary capitalist society, for example, opposite the people stand the reactionary imperialist upper strata.

In socialist society the entire population—the working class, peasants and intelligentsia—are the people.

40

The People As the Makers of History

The decisive significance of the people in the historical process stems from the determinative role played by the mode of production in society's development. Material production, as we have learned earlier, is the basis of social life, and the working people are the chief productive force. The working people consequently are the *decisive force* in social development, the *real makers* of history.

In what way is the people's role in history manifested?

The working people make history first and foremost by their productive labour. It is they who create all the material wealth: the towns and villages, factories and mills, roads and bridges, motors and machines, clothing and footwear, food and household utensils, in a word, everything without which we could not exist.

The people are the main driving force of technical progress. Painstakingly and perseveringly, from day to day, from year to year, from century to century, often unaware of it themselves, they devised and perfected the implements of labour, and this in the final count led to radical technical revolutions, to changes in the productive forces. The development of the productive forces, in its turn, has brought about a change in the mode of production as a whole. Even under the most onerous oppression, the labour of the ordinary people created the material prerequisites for mankind's progress, for the transition to a new social system.

The people's role in history, however, is not limited to developing the productive forces and thereby preparing the material conditions for the transition to a new social system. The people are also the *main force* which decides the fate of social revolutions, of political and national liberation movements. The class struggle, above all the working people's struggle against their oppressors, of which the social revolution is the highest form, serves as the driving force in the development of antagonistic class societies. Slave uprisings undermined the foundations of slave-owning society and were a prime cause of the transition to feudalism. The peasants and the urban poor were an important driving force in the bourgeois revolutions as a result of which feudalism gave way to the more progressive, capitalist system.

In pre-socialist societies the people did not enjoy the fruits of their labour and struggle, but their work and struggle were the principal factors which ultimately led to their emancipation and the rise of the advanced, socialist system.

The people have made a tremendous contribution to the development of mankind's spiritual culture. "The people," Maxim Gorky wrote, "are not merely the force which has created all material values; they are the exclusive and inexhaustible source of spiritual values; they are the first and foremost philosopher and poet in point of time, beauty and genius, the creator of all the great poems that exist, all the tragedies in the world, and, greatest among these tragedies, the history of world culture."

The people's labour, their creative endeavours are wellsprings of science and culture. Many prominent scientists and writers, artists and other leading figures in the field of culture whose great creations have enriched mankind, have come from among the ordinary people. The people create remarkable epic poems and fairy tales, songs and dances which bring the greatest enjoyment.The most outstanding artists have always taken the models for their finest works from the inexhaustible treasure-house of folk art.

By producing everything necessary for man to live and work, the people provide mental workers with *time* to engage in intellectual activities. Finally, the masses create and improve *language* without which communication among men and, consequently, social activity, science, culture and art are inconceivable.

Growing Role of the People in Historical Development

The people make history; they do not make it at will, but in accordance with the objective conditions, and, above all, with the mode of production which is historically determined. Since material production constantly develops from the lower to the higher, the people's role in the historical process also changes. Moreover, *as mankind progressively develops, the people's role in history rises*. Marxism has established that the deeper the social transformations and the more important the tasks facing society, the *larger* is the number of people taking part in the historical process and the *greater is their activity*. "Together with the thoroughness of the historical action," Marx and Engels wrote, "the size of the mass whose action it is will... increase."*

In slave-owning and feudal socio-economic formations the working people were deprived of the most elementary human rights; their creative powers had no outlet and, consequently, could not display themselves to the full. The slave-owners and feudal lords monopolised the state administration, politics, science and art, and kept the people in darkness and ignorance, dooming them to unbearable toil. The people's activity in those

---

* Karl Marx and Frederick Engels, "The Holy Family", in: Karl Marx, Frederick Engels, *Collected Works*, Vol. 4, Moscow, 1975, p. 82.

days was relatively restricted and their disunited and spontaneous actions against the exploiters were ruthlessly suppressed. At that time, as Lenin noted, history could only crawl at a painfully slow pace.

The material prerequisites for the emancipation of the working people from exploitation are created under capitalism. Large-scale machine production appears along with the proletariat, the class capable of leading the people in the fight against capitalism and achieving the victory of socialism. This class creates the Communist party which is guided by the theory of Marxism-Leninism and heads the revolutionary struggle of the working people. For these reasons the people play a bigger part in life under capitalism. Millions upon millions of working people are drawn into active political struggle and this considerably accelerates the course of history.

The working people are the main driving force in the socialist revolution. In contrast to preceding revolutions in which the people simply destroyed the old social system, in the course of the socialist revolution they not only demolish the old, capitalist society, but also create the new, socialist society.

The activity of the people and their role in social affairs are especially great under socialism. Socialism is consistent with the fundamental interests of the people, and that is why they are vitally concerned with building it. "Living, creative socialism is the product of the masses themselves," Lenin wrote.* *Greater activity of the people in building a new life is a law of socialist development.* This has been strikingly displayed in the Soviet Union, the first country in which socialism triumphed.

The role of the people in socialist conditions greatly increases mainly due to the *very nature of the socialist system,* the dominance of socialist production relations. Socialist ownership, which is now firmly established in socialist countries, unites, welds together all sections of the working people and ensures their active participation in building socialism.

Only socialism promotes the harmonious combination of social and personal interests and stimulates the material interest of the working people in the results of their labour. In capitalist society the working people produce great material and spiritual values, and are the main participants in all progressive social movements but the great part of the fruits of their labour, their struggle and efforts are appropriated by a handful of exploiters. The situation is different in socialist society: here the workers are vitally interested in strengthening and developing the socialist system because it is the

---

* V.I. Lenin, "Meeting of the All-Russia Central Executive Committee, November 1917", *Collected Works,* Vol. 26, p. 288.

basis of their political freedom, material wellbeing and cultural progress. The people are aware that they work for themselves, for their own society, and this is the source of their enthusiasm for work, stimulates their initiative, pioneering endeavours and mass socialist emulation.

The people's role under socialism increases also because of the *immensity of the tasks* confronting them. The victory of communism will signify a gigantic leap in society's development, it will be a result of vast, unparalleled changes in all spheres of social life; and all this is absolutely inconceivable without the energetic participation of the millions of working people. The Soviet people are renowned for their heroism and labour exploits.

In the most difficult conditions they secured the historic victory of socialism.They safeguarded the gains of socialism and saved humanity from enslavement in the titanic stuggle against the nazi invaders in the Great Patriotic War of 1941-1945. They rehabilitated the war-ruined economy made further progress in their creative labour, built a developed socialist society.

Leadership by the Communist Party of the Soviet Union is a primary factor of the people's enhancing role in socialist society. The Party equips the Soviet people with a scientific policy which is based on objective laws and takes into account the requirements of society's material life. Acting on the basis of the current production level, of the real possibilities, the Party sets the people further tasks and indicates the ways and means of accomplishing them. The Party educates the people constantly, stimulates their activities and seeks to enlist them on an ever wider scale in building the new society.

The masses are the decisive political force of our age. Proof of this are the unprecedented successes of the Soviet people, the enormous creative enthusiasm of the peoples of other socialist countries who are building socialism, the vigorous participation of the working people in capitalist states in the struggle for democracy, social progress and socialism, and the further deepening of the national liberation movement of the peoples in the developing countries. In our day the labouring masses are ardent and consistent champions of world peace. Their struggle for peace seriously impedes the efforts of the imperialist forces to unleash another world war.

2. Society and the Individual

The masses are not an abstract category. They include many millions of individuals. In order to understand what an individual is, it is necessary first to establish what is a man, for *individual means personality, a concrete human being.*

The Human Essence

Efforts to disclose the human essence were made long before Marx. But nothing came of them because philosophers entertained idealistic views of society's development. It cannot be denied, however, that 18th-century French Enlighteners and materialists conjectured that man was a product of the environment and circumstances, but at the same time they regarded the social environment as a modification of human ideas. Pre-Marxist social views therefore spun in a vicious circle: man, his thoughts and emotions were a product of the environment, while the environment was a result of the same human thoughts and emotions. This gave rise to the cult of the abstract man or "man in general", independent of time and space, a biological being connected with other individuals only through natural, biological relations.

Marx held an opposite view, namely that the human essence was *social.* Of course, nature provided the necessary biological material for the rise of man, but the transformation of this material into a human being, a human organism was brought about by social factors, and primarily by labour, by productive activity. Labour, as we said earlier, created man and also found its embodiment in the structure of the human body. Man became man not because he consists of organs, tissue and cells, because he breathes with lungs and nurses children with milk, but because he can *work, think* and *speak,* create implements of labour with which he transforms the surrounding world, nature and is capable of entering into social relations with other people.

In the course of his own development, from birth to death, the individual is *humanised* and *socialised,*i.e., he acquires human qualities per se, and comes to know his social environment that has been created by the labour and struggle of countless generations. Man cannot act in that environment and assimilate its achievements and experience in isolation from other people. He becomes socialised under the influence of his relations with other people, i. e., social relations, of which he is always a link.

The Individual

Marx and Engels rejected an abstract approach to man. They showed that man is always a *concrete individual,* and belongs to an historically determined social formation, class, nation, a working collective, etc.

In addition to qualities common to all people such as the ability to work, think, communicate with other people by means of language, etc., the *concrete man*, or *individual* possesses the qualities of the collective to which he belongs (nation, class, party, a production collective). Besides, a concrete individual has personal qualities which together with the qualities mentioned above make him what he is, namely a concrete individual. Individual qualities disclose his personality from all sides—education, occupation, skill, cultural level, family status, etc.

Numerous manifestations of life, and qualities of an individual are formed under the influence of social relations. Concrete social production and economic relations give rise to such *social types of individual* as slave or slave-owner, peasant or feudal lord, worker or capitalist and so forth.

Through their vehicles (class, nation, etc.) class, national and other relations inherent in society give rise to class, national and other peculiarities of the individual which are in fact a manifestation of his *social* life. For instance, the working class moulds such qualities as consciousness, organisation, discipline, integrity, intolerance of capitalism and bourgeois ideology, revolutionary spirit and so on in the individual that belongs to it.

The economic and social relations predominant in society and its spiritual culture, particularly its dominating ideas form manifestations of the individual's intellectual life—his thoughts and emotions, character, interests and aims.

In their unity an individual's qualities, i. e., his diverse vital manifestations—economic, social and spiritual—are a product and an expression of the totality of diverse social relations. "The essence of man," wrote Marx, "is no abstraction inherent in each single individual. In its reality it is the ensemble of the social relations."*

A concrete man, an individual, as we have seen, is a product of the social environment, of the society in which he lives and develops. At the same time one may well ask: why are there so many different individuals in one and the same society and why does one or another individual embody only some of the features of the given society, and not in equal measure at that?

The fact of the matter is that any society is *heterogeneous*. It includes vestiges of the old, the foundations of the present and the embryos of future social relations. For instance, under socialism there are vestiges of the old, capitalist division of labour and the survivals of the past in the conscious-

---

* Karl Marx, "Theses on Feuerbach", in: Karl Marx, Frederick Engels, *Collected Works*, Vol. 5, p. 4.

ness of people. Since the given society is heterogeneous it is natural that man is influenced by its different qualities. And though the decisive role in the formation of the individual is played by the relations which are predominant in society, man may also come under the influence of the survivals of the old socio-economic relations which breed in him feelings that are incompatible with the demands of the given society.

The society in which an individual lives and develops does not exist in isolation from societies of a different socio-economic and spiritual character. For instance, capitalism exists alongside socialism in the present epoch. And, obviously enough, in view of the very extensive development of the mass media and intensive inter-state relations alien ideas of bourgeois society penetrate the socialist world. This is yet another reason why there are individuals whose deeds and thoughts do not fully conform to social demands.

An important reason for the existence of a multitude of different individuals is that each of them lives and develops both in the given social environment (society in general) and in a *micro-environment,* i. e., in *his direct environment,* which includes the family, school, production collective, street, and so forth. The *micro-environment* is the prism through which the influence of the general social environment—economic and social relations, spiritual culture—is refracted. Thanks to the infinite diversity of concrete conditions making up the micro-environment, there is an endless number of variations and gradations in the make-up of the individual who comes from a common social environment, which can be explained only on the basis of an all-round investigation of these conditions.

Finally, another reason for the existence of numerous individuals in one and the same society is that an individual is an *active being.* The measure of his activity depends on the nature of the society in general and of the micro-environment in which he acts, and also on his personal qualities, experience, cultural level and his specific anatomical, physiological and psychic qualities (willpower, character, etc.). A concrete individual does not passively assimilate the influence of the social environment, but does so *actively* and *selectively,* in keeping with his specific personal qualities, interests, requirements and aims.

Being a product of the social environment the individual does not dissolve in society; he is not merely a cog in the social mechanism. He forms society to the same extent as social conditions form him. It should not be forgotten that it is people who change conditions.

Let us now see how people change conditions or, in other words, what role the individual plays in history.

3. The Role of the Individual in History

Because Marxists recognise historical necessity, bourgeois ideologists often accuse them of denying the role of individuals, of great people, of leaders, in history. These accusations are unfounded, for Marxism far from underestimates the role of the individual. Although Marxists maintain that individuals cannot change the objective course of history at will, they admit that the individual plays no small part in social development. "The idea of historical necessity," Lenin noted, "does not in the least undermine the role of the individual in history: all history is made up of the actions of individuals, who are undoubtedly active figures."* Only Marxism has demonstrated the real importance of the individual in social development and has also indicated the conditions in which the individual can play an important part in history.

An individual makes history by his labour, political activity, will and reason, and the greater is social progress the greater the influence of the individual on society. With the development of history, the deepening and extension of historical tasks, and the progress of science, technology and culture more and more people participate in historical events and each individual plays a mounting role in the historical process and increases his contribution to the treasure-store of material and spiritual culture. The creative activity of the individual is particularly great in socialist society where there are favourable conditions for free labour and activity in various spheres of social life.

The Role of Leaders in History

We know that the people, the masses make history. The people are divided into classes, which in the course of the class struggle organise their own political parties from whose ranks come leaders, the most experienced, trained and active members. The role of these leaders in history consists in forming parties and organising the people, rousing them to action, setting them definite tasks and mobilising them to carry out these tasks.

The more active the parties and the masses in history are and the wider the circle of people who influence social life the more pressing is the need for experienced, mature leaders. Without leaders the advanced class and its vanguard are incapable of gaining political power, maintaining and

---

* V.I. Lenin, "What the 'Friends of the People' Are and How They Fight the Social-Democrats", *Collected Works*, Vol. 1, p. 159.

consolidating its political rule, building its own state and fighting their political enemies successfully. "Not a single class in history has achieved power, without producing its political leaders, its prominent representatives able to organise a movement and lead it,"* Lenin wrote.

The role of leaders, of ideologists is particularly great in the proletariat's revolutionary movement. For the proletariat, organisation and iron discipline, unity and cohesion are the most important means for achieving the aims confronting it. And an organisation is inconceivable without experienced and battle-hardened leaders. Without highly authoritative leaders, intrepid organisers and wise ideologists, the working-class movement could not have found the right ways and means of fighting the exploiters.

Why Outstanding Personalities Appear and What is the Source of Their Strength

Great people do not appear by chance but by historical necessity, when the corresponding objective conditions are ripe. Outstanding political figures, leaders of the people, come to the fore in a period of radical revolutionary changes in society, very great political actions and popular uprisings. Men of genius appear in science most often when production requires some great scientific discovery. Great artists, as a rule, display their talent at the most significant turning points in history. Moreover, a talented person will go down in history only if his talent, character and intellect are needed by society at a given stage of its development.

Many names are recorded in history, but far from all of them were really great. There were men who acted contrary to historical necessity and sought to set the clock back. These men, by expressing the interests of reactionary classes, inevitably suffered defeat together with the evil cause they championed.

A man can be *truly* great only if he dedicates his life and energies to society's progress, if he, without sparing any effort, works for the new, the progressive, and tirelessly helps the advanced classes of society to introduce a progressive social systerm.

Why is an outstanding personality capable of accomplishing such great and difficult tasks? What is the source of his strength?

An outstanding personality's strength lies above all in the strength of the progressive social movement which he champions and leads. A great man is great because he understands the objective course of the historical process, sees the requirements of society's development and knows how to

---

* V.I. Lenin, "The Urgent Tasks of Our Movement", *Collected Works*, Vol. 4, p. 470.

satisfy these requirements, how to improve social life. An outstanding personality is strong because he serves the interests of the advanced classes, the people, and therefore enjoys their trust and support.

The personal qualities of a great man are of no small importance. Only a man endowed with uncommon abilities and personal qualities—great intellect, inexhaustible energy, resolution and bravery—can cope with the tasks history sets him. The fuller the personal qualities of a great man correspond to social needs, the more notable and important is his role in history.

The leaders of the proletariat and all the working people, Marx, Engels and Lenin, were outstanding personalities who left a deep imprint on history. They were leaders of a qualitatively new type, splendid theoreticians and organisers of the greatest movement, the revolutionary movement of the proletariat. They had resolution and bravery, unshakable conviction in the justice of the communist cause, love for the people and hatred for their enemies. They were closely bound up with the people, taught them and in turn learned from the people, generalising their rich revolutionary experience.

The great cause initiated by them is being successfully continued by their disciples and followers, prominent leaders of the Communist and Workers' parties who are heading the most powerful movement of our age, the people's movement towards socialism.

Marxism-Leninism recognises the big part played by outstanding personalities in history; at the same time it is incompatible with the personality cult, the blind worship of a great man allegedly endowed with superhuman ability to make history at his own will. The personality cult runs counter to socialist ideology and seriously harms the communist movement. Marx, Engels and Lenin always opposed the personality cult and exaggeration of the role of individual leaders as well as showering praise and flattery on them. The founders of Marxism-Leninism held that only collective leadership ensures the revolutionary movement's success.

The personality cult is harmful because it belittles both the people's role as makers of history and the role of the Communist Party and its central bodies as the collective leader of the people. It fetters the development of the Party's ideological life and the creative energies of the people, and accustoms them to passively waiting for orders from above. The personality cult and the consequent violations of the Leninist norms of Party and state life, of socialist law and democracy are alien to the democratic nature of socialism which is characterised by sovereignty of the people, and not by the omnipotence of one individual. That was why the CPSU condemned the personality cult and resolutely liquidated its consequences.

While resolutely condemning the personality cult, Marxism-Leninism holds that it would be wrong and harmful to confuse it with the authority of leaders. Lenin wrote that "the working class, which all over the world is waging a hard and persistent struggle for complete emancipation, needs authorities."* Marxism-Leninism calls for safeguarding the authority of leaders devoted to the people and to the Party.

All historical development shows that however great an individual is, he is incapable of determining the course of history. It is the people who make history and social revolutions and produce all the material and spiritual wealth of humanity.

* V.I. Lenin, "Preface to the Russian Translation of K. Kautsky's Pamphlet: *The Driving Forces and Prospects of the Russian Revolution*", *Collected Works*, Vol. 11, p. 412.

CHAPTER IV

Classes and the Class Struggle

In the previous chapter we showed that the working people are the chief and decisive force in society's development Society, however, is not homogeneous, it is made up of definite classes, social groups and social sections.

What are classes and what is their role in social development? This question is answered by the Marxist-Leninist theory of classes and the class struggle.

1. The Essence and Origin of Classes

Scholars knew that people were divided into classes and that the class struggle existed in society before the birth of Marxism. But, being idealists in their understanding of social life, they were unable to find the objective basis for the division of society into classes. They did not see that the reason for the class division of society should be sought in material production, the principal sphere of human activity.

A comprehensive definition of classes was given by Lenin in his work *A Great Beginning*. "Classes," he wrote, "are large groups of people differing from each other by the place they occupy in a historically determined system of social production, by their relation (in most cases fixed and formulated in law) to the means of production, by their role in the social organisation of labour, and, consequently, by the dimensions of the share of social wealth of which they dispose and the mode of acquiring it."*

The relation of a class to the means of production is its chief feature determining its place and role in social production, and also the way it obtains its income and the size of that income.

The division of society into classes is not eternal. In primitive society, there were no classes. Production was at such a low level that it yielded only means of subsistence barely enough to keep the people from starvation. There was no possibility for accumulating material wealth, for the birth of private property, classes and exploitation.

* V.I. Lenin, "A Great Beginning", *Collected Works*, Vol. 29, p. 421.

Subsequently, however, as the productive forces developed and labour productivity increased, people began to produce more than they consumed. It became possible to accumulate material wealth and appropriate means of production. Private property appeared, as a result of the increasing division of labour and growth of trade.

The development of private property in place of communal property increased the people's economic inequality. Some men, mainly the tribal nobility, became rich and seized the communal means of production. Others, deprived of the means of production, were compelled to work for those who became their owners. This was how the disintegration and the class stratification of the primitive community took place. This process was consummated in the birth of opposing classes and exploitation.

Classes arose when the primitive-communal system began to disintegrate and the slave-owning system began to take root. The antithetical position of classes in society was the source of their bitter struggle. For many centuries the class struggle was the primary feature in the development of mankind.

2. The Class Struggle as the Source of Development of Antagonistic Class Societies

The history of antagonistic class societies is the history of the class struggle. "Freeman and slave, patrician and plebeian, lord and serf, guild-master and journeyman, in a word, oppressor and oppressed, stood in constant opposition to one another, carried on an uninterrupted, now hidden, now open fight, a fight that each time ended, either in a revolutionary re-constitution of society at large, or in the common ruin of the contending classes."*

The struggle of antagonistic classes is irreconcilable because of the basic differences in their economic and political status in society. For countless centuries the working people, whether slaves, peasants or industrial workers, have been brutally exploited by the ruling classes and it is natural that they should struggle against oppression and strive for a free and happy life.

A class society has basic and non-basic classes. The *basic classes* are those connected with the mode of production prevailing in society. In an antagonistic class society they are, on the one hand, the class owning the means of production and, on the other, the oppressed class standing in

* Karl Marx andFrederick Engels, "Manifesto of the Communist Party", in: Karl Marx, Frederick Engels, *Collected Works*, Vol. 6, p. 482.

opposition to it. Slaves and slave-owners in slave-owning society, peasants and feudal lords under feudalism, the proletariat and the bourgeoisie under capitalism—these are the basic classes in antagonistic societies.

Antagonistic societies also have *non-basic classes* which are not directly connected with the prevailing mode of production (free artisans in slave-owning society, peasants in capitalist society and others), and also various social groups (the intelligentsia, clergy and others).

The class struggle in an antagonistic society takes place above all between the basic social classes. The non-basic classes and social groups usually have no line of their own in this struggle, vacillate and in the long run side with one of the basic antagonistic classes and defend its interests.

The class struggle is a mighty driving force, the source of development of an antagonistic class society This struggle determines the development of an antagonistic society both in relatively "peaceful" periods and particularly in periods of revolutionary storms and upheavals.

In capitalist conditions the class struggle is an important factor in the development of the productive forces. Were it not for the struggle of the workers, for example, the capitalists would be less concerned with the development of technology. It would be much simpler and cheaper for them to extract profit by such tried and tested methods as prolonging the working day and cutting wages. But the stubborn struggle of the workers, in addition to competition between the capitalists, forces the latter to introduce new machinery and advance technology. "…Almost all the new inventions were the result of collisions between the worker and the employer…. After each new strike of any importance, there appeared a new machine," Marx wrote.*

The class struggle is even more important in the political life of an antagonistic society. The struggle of the working class in the present period, for example, undermines the positions of imperialism. It is an important obstacle in the way of the imperialists' aggressive schemes, of their efforts to crush the national liberation movement, truncate or eliminate democratic freedoms and thereby retard society's progressive development.

Without the class struggle there would be no social progress. Society's progressive development is usually faster, the more stubborn and organised is the struggle of the exploited against the exploiters. The social revolution, the highest form of the class struggle, plays a particularly great part in

---

* Karl Marx, "The Poverty of Philosophy", in: Karl Marx, Frederick Engels, *Collected Works*, Vol. 6, p. 188.

social progress and results in the destruction of the old and the establish-ment of a new, more progressive social system.

The history of class-divided societies is one of struggle between the exploited and the exploiters.

There was a bitter struggle between the slaves and the slave-owners in slave-owning society which took on the most diverse forms from breaking tools to mass uprisings, like that led by Spartacus (first century B. C.) involving more than 100,000 slaves.

The class struggle intensified under feudalism, where the peasants and the feudal lords were the main contending classes, and the urban working people, specifically the artisans, often sided with the peasants. Uprisings turned into peasant wars in which hundreds of thousands of people were involved. These wars often spread over vast territories and lasted for many years, like Wat Tyler's Revolt in England (14th century), the Jacquerie in France (14th-15th centuries), the peasant War in Germany (16th century) the uprisings headed by Bolotnikov and Razin (17th century) and Pugachev (18th century) in Russia, the Taiping Rebellion in China (19th century) and so on.

The uprisings of the oppressed in slave-owning and feudal societies, however, could not put an end to exploitation, because the conditions were not yet ripe for this. The level of production did not permit the shift to a system without exploitation and oppression. These uprisings were sponta-neous and at times the rebels had no clear idea either of the common aims of the struggle or the ways of achieving them and went into battle either under a religious banner or with slogans demanding a "good monarch". They had no progressive theory to illuminate their road, nor their own party. As we shall see later, these conditions are only created under capitalism.

Nevertheless, the slave and peasant uprisings played a big and progres-sive part in history. The slaves undermined the mainstays of slave-owning society, and the serfs were one of the principal forces which brought about the fall of feudalism and the transition to the more progressive capitalist system.

3. The Class Struggle in Capitalist Society

*The Struggle Between the Bourgeoisie
and the Proletariat—a Law of Capitalist Development*

The bourgeoisie and the proletariat are the basic classes in capitalist society. In its quest of profit the bourgeoisie exploits the proletariat and this exploitation is intensified as capitalism develops. The worker's labour is increasingly speeded up and he is reduced to a mere appendage of the machine. The proletariat especially suffers from such intrinsic features of capitalism as economic and financial crises, unemployment and predatory wars.

The proletariat naturally cannot reconcile itself to all this. The nature of capitalism which robs the worker of the fruits of his labour, and the worker's position in society, impel him to fight the bourgeoisie. The history of capitalist society is, therefore, the history of struggle between the proletariat and the bourgeoisie. This struggle is law-governed and is the primary source of capitalist development. The struggle of the proletariat against the bourgeoisie becomes especially intense in the epoch of imperialism when the economic and political contradictions of capitalism become extremely acute.

It is the proletariat's mission to *abolish exploitation and capitalism and build a classless communist society.* No other social class is able to fulfil this great and lofty task, for owing to their objective positions none of them is consistently revolutionary.

The bourgeoisie was revolutionary only when it fought the feudal lords for domination in society. But having gained power it becomes more and more reactionary, and now its sole aim is to perpetuate exploitation.

The middle sections, in particular the peasants and artisans who are quite numerous under capitalism, are also not revolutionary to the end. They hold no independent position in society and, with the development of capitalism, they become stratified. The majority of the peasants and artisans are reduced to ruin and join the ranks of the proletariat; and a negligible number break their way into the capitalist class. In the fierce class struggle the peasants vacillate. The proletariat, therefore, has the task of winning them over to its side and making them its reliable allies.

The intelligentsia (engineers and technicians, doctors, teachers, scientists and others) cannot be consistently revolutionary either. The intelligentsia is not a class and is not homogeneous. Its top echelon is recruited from the ruling classes and faithfully serves the bourgeoisie, while the bulk of the intellectuals are hired workers whose status is close to that of the working class, but they are more susceptible to the influence of bourgeois ideology.

The proletariat is the only consistently revolutionary class in capitalist society. It is connected with the most progressive form of production, machine industry, and is constantly growing and developing. The very nature of capitalist production helps unite, organise and educate the working class. In fighting for its liberation, the proletariat is capable of organising and leading all other working people who share its hatred for the capitalist system. By emancipating itself, it emancipates all other working people and aɒol'shes for ever exploitation of man by man. On gaining victory, it returns to the working people everything they produce, eliminating thereby the greatest social injustice—a social system in which a handful of oppressors appropriate the fruits of labour of the millions.

Forms of the Class Struggle of the Prolerariat

As capitalism develops so does the proletariat and the forms of its struggle against the bourgeoisie become more diverse and acute. There are three main forms of the proletariat's class struggle—economic, political and ideological.

Economic struggle, the effort of the proletariat to improve material and working conditions, is the simplest form most accessible to the workers.They demand higher wages, better working conditions, shorter hours and so on from the employers and if these demands are not met they go on strike.

The economic struggle, historically the first form of the proletariat's class struggle, plays a big part in the development of the revolutionary movement. It helps to draw the mass of workers into the class struggle and serves as a good school of organisation for them. The class awareness of the workers and their class solidarity grow in the course of this struggle, and the first workers' organisations—trade unions, co-operatives, mutual aid funds—appear.

At the same time the economic struggle has a limited character. It is not yet the struggle of the entire working class against the bourgeoisie as a class, but clashes of groups of workers with one capitalist at a factory in a particular district or with several capitalists in one or another branch of production. Moreover—and this is the main thing—it does not affect the basis of capitalism, private property, and does not aim to overthrow the political rule of the bourgeoisie. The purpose of this struggle is not to abolish exploitation, but merely to restrict and mitigate it.

With the growth of the proletariat, the economic struggle of the workers in individual factories and districts merges into the common struggle of the working class against the capitalist class as a whole. The class struggle enters its higher, political form.

Political struggle is, in the final analysis, the struggle for the demolition of the mainstays of the capitalist system, for state power, for a working-class state.

Through economic struggle the proletariat can somewhat improve its material conditions and wrest some economic concessions from the bourgeoisie. But it can satisfy its fundamental economic and political interests and abolish exploitation forever only by destroying the political rule of the bourgeoisie and establishing its own power.

It is to achieve this aim that the proletariat wages the political struggle, employing the most diverse means: political strikes and demonstrations, peaceful parliamentary struggle and armed struggle. All these means, however, are in the final count subordinated to preparing and carrying out the socialist revolution. The socialist, proletarian revolution is the highest stage in the class struggle of the proletariat, a decisive and sole means of abolishing capitalism and winning political power.

Of great importance in the proletariat's revolutionary movement is the *ideological struggle,* i. e., the struggle against bourgeois ideology which dominates in capitalist society, and the struggle for the victory of the socialist, proletarian ideology.

The development of capitalism inevitably solidifies and organises the proletariat. But to abolish the capitalist system the proletariat must not only organise as a class, but also become conscious of its class interests, of its great historic mission. For this, revolutionary theory is needed. Due to the lack of sufficient time, means and adequate education, the proletariat was unable to create this theory. It was elaborated by intellectuals who sided with the proletariat. This new revolutionary theory was created by Marx, Engels and Lenin.

The task, however, was not only to elaborate a progressive revolutionary theory, it was necessary to spread it among the workers. Ideological struggle is consequently a struggle against spontaneity in the working-class movement, struggle for the mastery of advanced Marxist-Leninist ideology by the working masses.

Marxist-Leninist theory is constantly being attacked by bourgeois ideologists, reformists and revisionists. Therefore, the effort to keep the Marxist-Leninist theory pure and to defend it from all enemies, above all from the ideology of imperialist reaction, is also a part of the ideological struggle.

Like the economic struggle, the ideological struggle is not an aim in itself; it is subordinated to political tasks, those of overthrowing the bourgeoisie and bringing the proletariat to power.

The Marxist Party As the Organiser and Leader
of the Proletariat's Class Struggle

Only the political party of the proletariat can competently lead the working people's class struggle and properly combine all its forms. The party's role is particularly great in the imperialist era when, owing to the extreme aggravation of capitalist contradictions, the socialist revolution becomes an immediate practical task.

The parties of the Second International which favoured reforms and compromise with the bourgeoisie were unable to provide proper leadership to the proletarian movement in the new historical conditions. A party of a new type, a revolutionary, Marxist party was needed and such a party was founded by Lenin.

The Marxist party is the *advanced revolutionary* detachment of the proletariat, its vanguard. As the highest form of organisation of the proletariat, it rallies together all its other organisations (trade unions, co-operatives, etc.), gives them a political leadership and concentrates their efforts on the single goal of overthrowing capitalism and building socialist society. "By educating the workers' party," Lenin wrote, "Marxism educates the vanguard of the proletariat, capable of assuming power and *leading the whole people* to socialism, of directing and organising the new system, of being the teacher, the guide, the leader of all the working and exploited people in organising their social life without the bourgeoisie and against the bourgeoisie."*

The Marxist party is capable of fulfilling its mission as the vanguard, the advanced detachment of the working class and leader of the entire people because it is equipped with scientific Marxist theory, knowledge of the laws of social development and knows how to apply these laws to secure the revolutionary transformation of society.

As the advanced, politically *conscious* detachment of the proletariat, the party constantly develops the workers' socialist consciousness and protects the working class from the influence of decaying bourgeois ideology; the party wages an implacable struggle against any attempt to falsify or "revise" Marxism. It develops Marxist theory on the basis of the latest scientific achievements and the practical experience of society.

The Marxist party is the advanced, conscious and *organised* detachment of the working class bound by a common desire to apply the revolutionary ideas of Marxism-Leninism in practice. The party is intolerant of all kinds

* V.I. Lenin, "The State and Revolution", *Collected Works*, Vol. 25, p. 409.

of opportunists who seek to destroy its unity, to undermine it from within and render it incapable of leading the proletariat's class struggle.

The Marxist party is a genuine people's party; it unites the finest representatives of the people and it is bound by thousands of threads with the working people. By expressing the people's innermost aspirations and selflessly defending their vital interests, the party enjoys their confidence and support. The Marxist party draws its invincible strength and support from its close ties with the people.

Such a truly revolutionary, people's party is the Communist Party of the Soviet Union which was founded by Lenin.

The Bankruptcy of Bourgeois and Opportunistic Theories of Classes and Class Struggle

In contrast to the Marxist theory of classes and the class struggle, bourgeois ideologists preach class peace under capitalism. They especially persist in denying the existence of classes and the class struggle in contemporary bourgeois society.

Some bourgeois sociologists declare that in present-day capitalist society there is neither exploitation nor hostile classes, that there are only social groups according to profession, education, income, age, religious and political views and a number of other features. No property relations apparently connect people belonging to these groups, and relations between them are completely harmonious. A man can easily move from one group to another at will.

Other bourgeois sociologists admit that classes exist, but maintain that in modern bourgeois society class distinctions are being eliminated and classes are gradually converging into one huge "middle" class. They say, for example, that very shortly everyone in the United States will belong to this "middle" class, and that in present-day America it is difficult to find any difference between exploiters and exploited.

The ideologists of the bourgeoisie claim that the workers are no longer proletarians, that their standard of living is high, they have savings and buy shares, and therefore. like the factory owners, get the profits. On the other hand, the rights of employers are supposedly becoming more and more restricted by the state, as a result of which they play a smaller part in production.

The fables that there are no classes and no class struggle in comtemporary bourgeois society invented by capitalism's apologists are echoed by reformists and revisionists who insist that there are no classes in the present-day capitalist society, that "all are workers" there, and that in the final analysis the interests of the farmers, industrial workers, business-men, office employees and intellectuals all coincide.

They brand Lenin's definition of classes as "obsolete" and replace it by concepts like "group", etc. People, they maintain, unite in groups not according to their relation to the means of production, but according to other, secondary considerations. By denying the existence of classes, the revisionists renounce the class struggle and believe that workers should not fight against the bourgeoisie in our day and age but must promote technical progress which will supposedly place power in the hands of the people automatically without the class struggle and revolution.

The apologists of the bourgeoisie and their reformist yes-men spread fraudulent theories about the absence of classes and the class struggle in contemporary bourgeois society and proclaim an era of "class peace", "social partnership" and "harmony of labour and capital", in order to mis-lead the working class, make the workers think that the class struggle against the bourgeoisie is futile and direct the working-class movement along the reformist path.

What is the actual state of affairs?

It is quite true that the standard of living of some workers in the U.S., above all the upper section, is high, particularly in comparison with that of the working class in other capitalist countries. But we must not forget that far from all American workers enjoy this high standard.

Can we talk seriously about the living standard of millions of unem-ployed while only 1% of the population of the United States owns a quarter of the national income and half of this 1% owns one-fifth?

In the face of these facts, how can they speak of the disappearance of classes, of the "great American middle class"! The United States is a coun-try of vast social contrasts and deep social contradictions. In most of the other capitalist countries the working people are in a much worse position than in the United States and the contradictions between the bourgeoisie and the proletariat are deeper and sharper.

It is beyond doubt that capitalist ownership prevails in contemporary bourgeois society; consequently there exist antagonistic classes, the bour-geoisie and the proletariat, and the fierce struggle between them continues.

The Class Struggle
in Contemporary Capitalist Society

The class struggle of the proletariat against the bourgeoisie in the capi-talist countries is now waged at a new stage of capitalism's general crisis, when the world socialist system is turning into the decisive factor of world development. This situation has now become more favourable for the working-class movement due to the successes of the Soviet Union and the entire world socialist system, the deepening of the crisis of world capitalism, the growing influence of the Communist parties among the people, and the ideological bankruptcy of reformism. The possibilities for the working-class movement have been further extended by the people's dissatisfaction with the reactionary policy of the imperialists, particularly the fanning of war psychosis and the arms race, the main brunt of which is borne by the people. More and more people are becoming convinced that socialism is the only way out of their predicament and this creates favourable conditions for drawing them into the active struggle against the bourgeoisie. The power of the proletarian movement is multiplied by the achievements of the socialist system, which clearly show socialism's advantages over capitalism. These achievements inspire the workers in the capitalist countries in their struggle and make them confident in the coming victory of socialism.

The struggle of the proletariat for socialism is now combined with the movement of the peoples for peace, national independence and democracy, and this is the main specific feature of the working-class movement today. We shall examine contemporary democratic movements in greater detail further on.

In the struggle for its rights, for democracy and socialism, the proletariat employs the most diverse methods: strikes, demonstrations, meetings, conferences and so on. It also resorts to parliamentary struggle.

The traditional form of struggle, the strike, is the most widely used method in present-day conditions. The fact that the strike movement in the capitalist countries is growing in size and strength refutes the assertions of bourgeois and reformist scribblers about the harmony of the interests of the bourgeoisie and the proletariat.

The demands of the workers, it should be noted, go beyond purely economic bounds and acquire a political character. The working class and its revolutionary vanguard, the Marxist parties, direct their main blow at the capitalist monopolies, the bulwark of reaction and aggression, which bear direct responsibility for the arms race and the hard lot of the working people.

A distinctive feature of the contemporary, working-class movement is that the workers acquire more and more allies in their anti-monopoly struggle. Their traditional ally is the *peasantry* which is a major political force. The *middle urban strata* (petty entrepreneurs, artisans and traders) are defending their interests with increasing determination. As a result of the scientific and technical revolution the army of hired labour is being steadily swelled by the *intelligentsia* whose interests are becoming more and more linked with the struggle of the working class for democracy and socialism. *Young people* are displaying increasing activity: realising that they have no future under capitalism, the progressive part of the young people and students fight not only for their own rights but also against the mainstays of capitalist society. Masses of women, and religious believers, also oppose the monopolies.

The exceptionally broadscale and considerable intensification of the political activity of the working people in the struggle against imperialist reaction, for peace, democracy and socialism is a typical feature of the contemporary working-class movement.

The growth of Communist and Workers' parties convincingly attests to the profound change that has taken place in the consciousness of the working people. More than 60 years ago, when the Bolshevik Party led by Lenin rallied the people for the battle against capitalism, there were only 400,000 Communists in the world. Now the communist movement has tens of millions of fighters and is the most massive and influential political force.

The reactionary imperialist circles employ the most brutal measures against the communist and democratic movement. They increasingly resort to methods of open dictatorship by the monopoly bourgeoisie, abolish the remaining elements of democracy and use an old means to suppress the people, a "strong-hand" government. Ominous symptoms of fascism are appearing in some capitalist countries.

The broadening of the social base of the revolutionary movement creates a firm foundation for the united anti-monopoly front. "In the course of anti-monopolist and anti-imperialist united action," states the Document of the International Meeting of Communist and Workers' Parties which took place in Moscow in 1969, "favourable conditions are created for uniting all democratic trends into a political alliance capable of decisively limiting the role played by the monopolies in the economies of the countries concerned, of putting an end to the power of big capital and of bringing about such radical political and economic changes as would ensure the most favourable conditions for continuing the struggle for socialism. The main force in this democratic alliance is the working class."*

Imperialist reaction and its henchmen in the labour movement, the anti-communist Right-wing Social-Democratic leaders and also opportunists of

* *International Meeting of Communist and Workers' Parties, Moscow 1969*, Prague, 1969, p. 27.

all shades, impede working-class unity, pursue a splitting policy, distort the essence of Marxist-Leninist theory and try to discredit the communist movement. In view of this, it has become highly important at the present stage to fight opportunist tendencies in the working-class and communist movement and resolutely overcome Right and "Left" revisionism inasmuch as neither the one nor the other is compatible with the basic principles of Marxism-Leninism.

Consistent defence of the unity of the international working-class and communist movement and prevention of any actions which could undermine this unity are necessary conditions for victory in the struggle for national independence, democracy and peace, for the successful accomplishment of the tasks of the socialist revolution and socialist construction.

4. Classes and the Class Struggle in the Transition Period from Capitalism to Socialism

We know that an implacable struggle has been going on between the exploited and the exploiters ever since the birth of private ownership of the means of production and antagonistic classes. This struggle ultimately leads to the socialist revolution, as a result of which the rule of the bourgeoisie is replaced by the government of the working people, the dictatorship of the proletariat. This ushers in the transition period from capitalism to socialism.

The Class Struggle During the Transition from Capitalism to Socialism

The class struggle in the period of transition from capitalism to socialism is inevitable. The overthrown bourgeoisie will not reconcile itself to its loss of power to the workers it has exploited for decades; the bourgeoisie will not forgive these people for having encroached on its holy of holies, private property. The bourgeoisie simply cannot believe that an end has come to its idle, carefree life which seemed eternal and inviolable, to its wealth, privileges and unlimited rule. That is why it resists the new, proletarian power so frenziedly and with such fanatical obstinacy.

In this period the bourgeoisie employs every means in the struggle against the proletariat. Making use of its economic positions, former ties with the top intellectuals, civil servants and army leaders, it tries to disrupt the country's economy, the functioning of state institutions and the defence. It also strives to influence the minds of the people. Lastly, in order to restore capitalism, it launches an overt armed struggle against the working people, placing its main hopes on the help of international capital. History (the campaign of fourteen imperialist powers against the young Soviet Republic, the intervention of the imperialists in Korea, Vietnam, the events in other countries, etc.) shows that the victorious proletariat is compelled to wage a bitter struggle not only against the capitalists of its own country but also against the reactionary international bourgeoisie.

In other words, the dictatorship of the proletariat does not eliminate the class struggle, which continues in the transition period as well. But this struggle is waged in conditions when the proletariat has political power and controls key positions in the economy. The forms of the class struggle change correspondingly."The dictatorship of the proletariat," Lenin wrote, "is not the end of the class struggle but its continuation in new forms. The dictatorship of the proletariat is class struggle waged by a proletariat that is victorious and has taken political power into its hands against a bourgeoisie that has been defeated but not destroyed, a bourgeoisie that has not vanished, not ceased to offer resistance but that has intensified its resistance."*

The new forms of the class struggle in the period of transition from capitalism to socialism are: suppression of the resistance of the exploiters and this does not exclude the use of force, struggle to emancipate the peasant from the influence of the bourgeoisie and draw him into socialist construction, enrollment of bourgeois specialists to work in the national economy, and educating the people in the spirit of socialist discipline.

The Attitude of the Proletariat to the Use of Force

The implacable struggle of the working class and the peasants against the defeated but resisting bourgeoisie is a major factor in social development in the transition period from capitalism to socialism. This struggle ultimately leads to the complete abolition of the social root of the bourgeoisie as a class and to the establishment of a society without exploitation of man by man.

What means does the working class use to overcome the resistance of the bourgeoisie and what is its attitude to the use of force?

Bourgeois ideologists portray the dictatorship of the proletariat as a reign of unrestricted terror and destruction and claim that the proletariat uses force, armed struggle, as the sole means of fighting the bourgeoisie. In reality, however Marxism-Leninism, both in theory and in practice, pro-

---

* V.I. Lenin, "Foreword to the Published Speech 'Deception of the People with Slogans of Freedom and Equality'", *Collected Works*, Vol. 29, p. 381.

ceeds from the principle that different methods, both forcible and peaceful, can be used to overcome the resistance of the bourgeoisie.

The proletariat is the most humane class of our age. It strives to preserve and to enhance the achievements of human culture, to raise the level of production and to protect the principal productive force—man, the working people. That is why the proletariat is vitally interested in peaceful transition from capitalism to socialism. The peaceful way safeguards huge material values, saves many human lives and therefore, as Lenin wrote, is the most painless, easiest and most advantageous path for the people to follow.

But whether the socialist revolution will develop peacefully or non-peacefully after the establishment of the dictatorship of the proletariat does not depend on the will of one or another class and even less so of an individual, but above all on the *objective correlation of class forces* in the given country, and particularly on the strength of the resistance of the bourgeoisie or on its willingness to make concessions.

If the forces of the victorious working class and its allies are far superior to the forces of the bourgeoisie, it will realise that armed resistance is futile and will prefer, as Lenin said, to "save its heads", and the revolution then can follow a peaceful path. If, on the other hand, the bourgeoisie does not submit to the demands of the new authority and resorts to arms in an attempt to reverse the course of history, the working class has no option other than to crush the resistance of the bourgeoisie by armed force, for in the circumstances this is the only thing it can do to safeguard its gains and the vital interests of all working people.

In the Soviet Union, the first country of the socialist revolution, the bourgeoisie tried to regain its lost power, property and privileges by force of arms and enlisted the armed assistance of international capital. In these conditions the working class had to resort to force to smash the bourgeoisie. The suppression of the bourgeoisie by force of arms, the civil war, was a specific form of the class struggle in the Soviet Republic during the transition period.

The experience of the European socialist countries, however, has shown that forcible suppression of the bourgeoisie is not always a necessary form of the class struggle in the transition period. There was no civil war in these countries because real power was on the side of the proletariat. The main positions of the reactionary forces in these countries had already been destroyed in the course of the liberation struggle against German fascism, while the remaining part of the bourgeoisie, not possessing sufficient strength, did not venture to offer armed resistance to the people's government.

The acuteness of the class struggle in the transition period differs not only from country to country, but also in one and the same country at different periods of its development. The experience of the Soviet Union and other socialist countries shows that as the dictatorship of the proletariat is consolidated and socialist construction makes headway, the balance of the class force steadily changes in favour of socialism with the result that the resistance offered by the remnants of the hostile classes grows weaker. This is the general tendency in the class struggle in a country in the transition period from capitalism to socialism.

Acting on the principle that the class struggle can acquire diverse forms in the transition period, the proletariat and its Marxist party set themselves the aim of mastering all forms of class struggle and applying those which best correspond to the concrete situation, to the objective correlation of the class forces.

5. The Class Composition of Socialist Society

With the completion of socialist construction in the Soviet Union, the class composition of Soviet society radically changed. Private ownership of the means of production and the exploitation of man by man were abolished forever. The exploiting classes disappeared both in town and country.

There remained two friendly classes, *the working class and the collective-farm peasantry,* plus the working *intelligentsia,* all of which basically changed in Soviet times.

The working class was no longer the proletariat which had been exploited and deprived of all rights under capitalism. Together with all the other people, it owns the means of production and is the true master of the country. The working class has grown numerically since the establishment of Soviet power: in 1978, it totalled 75.7 million people, compared with 9.8 million in 1913, 23.7 million in 1940 and 64.3 million in 1970. Its cultural, technical and educational standards have risen greatly and so has its political activity. Being the main productive force of the society and its most revolutionary, disciplined, organised and conscious class, the working class in developed socialist society holds the *leading place in the social structure, in the entire system of social relations.*

The collectivisation of agriculture and the cultural revolution changed the position of the Soviet peasants beyond recognition. From a disunited, downtrodden class, exploited by the landlords and kulaks, the peasants became a genuinely free class.

Collective labour for the benefit of the country brought the peasant out of his age-old isolation, helped him overcome his private-owner psychology and fostered a spirit of collectivism, friendship and cooperation in him. Its culture and technical knowledge grew immensely. The extensive use of modern machinery necessitated the training of large contingents of farm-machine operators whose labour differs little from that of the workers.

The intelligentsia too has changed greatly. The Soviet intelligentsia, the majority of whom come from the ranks of the working class and the peasants, is inseparable from the people and serves them loyally and selflessly. The ranks of the intelligentsia, particularly technical and scientific, are swelling rapidly as a result of the growth and improvement of production, and progress in science, technology and culture. In 1978 alone, the national economy received 1,999,000 specialists, of whom 771,500 had a higher education and 1,228,400 a specialised secondary education.

Class relations of domination and subordination have been abolished for ever in the Soviet Union; there are no privileged classes or groups in it and all members of society have an equal relation to the means of production; therefore exploitation, the appropriation of someone else's labour, is impossible. Each has an income that depends on the amount of work he puts in, and not on capital invested.

Since there are no exploiters and exploited but only working classes and social groups in socialist society, there is no class struggle. A solid alliance of the working class, the collective-farm peasantry and the people's intelligentsia has been formed.

The *social, political and ideological unity of the Soviet people* has been formed in socialist society. This unity has its source in the community of the basic economic and political aims of the working class, the peasants and the intelligentsia, in their unanimous striving to build communist society which will bring them the greatest material and cultural benefits. This community of interests enables the Soviet people to act together, harmoniously, in order to overcome by concerted effort the hardest trials and to accomplish tasks of great historic importance. The strength of millions of people, bound by their community of interests, welded together by unity of action, constitutes a great, indestructible force.

The class composition of Soviet society is *mobile:* it is moving from class differentiation towards social homogeneity, and class distinctions are being overcome.

6. Ways of Eliminating Class Distinctions

Socialist society has two friendly classes, the working class and the peasants. This is because under socialism two forms of socialist property—state and cooperative collective farm—are preserved, as a result of which essential distinctions between town and country remain. Under socialism there is also the intelligentsia, a large and important social group which owes its existence to the still surviving essential distinctions between manual and mental labour.

That is why the process of eliminating both class differences and the distinctions between the intelligentsia, on the one hand, and the workers and the peasants, on the other, actually entails the abolition of the distinctions between town and country, between mental and manual labour. The Party's policy is directed towards helping to bring the working class, the collective-farm peasantry and the intelligentsia closer together, and gradually erasing the essential distinctions between town and countryside and between brainwork and manual labour. This is one of the key sectors in the building of a classless society.

Social distinctions in Soviet society are gradually erased on the basis of the steady development of the productive forces and socialist production relations and their development into communist relations.

Ways of Eliminating the Essential Distinctions Between Town and Country

Under capitalism, the town ruthlessly exploits the country, and there is consequently an irreconcilable antithesis of interests. Socialism removed the antithesis between town and country, but essential distinctions between them remain as regards the economy, culture and way of life. The main reason is that in town, in industry, property belongs to the state, to the whole people, while in the countryside, in collective-farm production, group, co-operative and collective-farm property prevails. Moreover, the countryside is somewhat behind the town in the cultural level and its way of life differs.

In the course of building communism collective-farm property is further consolidated and developed, and gradually draws closer to the property of the whole people. This process takes place as the technical facilities of the collective farm grow, causing agricultural labour gradually to become a variety of industrial labour. Greater mechanisation steadily raises labour productivity and agriculture's efficiency, and this leads to a further increase in the incomes of the collective farms and the collective farmers. The amounts and the forms of labour remuneration received by the collective farmers are drawing closer to the amounts and forms of labour remuneration of urban workers at factories.

The changes in the nature of agricultural production alter the face of the countryside, improving the way of life of the peasants and raising their cultural standard. Inter-collective farm and state and co-operative associations specialising in the production or processing of specific types of farm products are being set up in the countryside. They greatly resemble urban industrial enterprises in terms of their technical equipment and the high qualification of their workers.

Large-scale construction of canteens, kindergartens and nursenes, bakeries, shops and various service establishments is underway in the rural areas. Housing construction has also assumed extensive proportions, and more and more urban-type houses with central heating, water supply, and all other amenities are being built. The collective farm villages are gradually turning into modern, urban-type settlements.

The collective farms are investing large funds in the construction of cultural centres, clubs, libraries, schools, stadiums, playgrounds, etc. The book and the radio, telephone and TV are permanent features of collective-farm life. Universities of culture, people's theatres, music schools, and amateur arts are increasingly spreading in rural areas.

Town and country are drawing together also as a result of the change in vocational composition of the population. A large number of engineers, technicians, agronomists, live-stock experts amd farm-machine operators work in the countryside. More and more teachers, doctors and other specialists serve rural areas. Living conditions of the urban population will greatly improve. The negative aspects of urban life will be eliminated, and people will have more air, light and greenery. In this respect their working and living conditions will draw closer to those in the countryside.

That is how the essential distinctions between town and country are being removed. Once this is achieved, the division of society into the working class and the peasantry will disappear forever.

Ways of Eliminating the Essential Distinctions Between Manual and Brain Workers

The vast majority of mental workers, intellectuals, have served the ruling classes for centuries and helped to oppress the working people, the manual workers. This further deepened the age-old antithesis between manual and mental labour. Socialism has abolished this antithesis as well. Soviet intellectuals are working for the good of their socialist country hand in hand with the manual workers, the workers and the peasants. Under socialism, however, essential distinctions between manual and brain workers still remain: the cultural and technical level of the workers and peasants still lags behind the cultural level and the technical knowledge of the intelligentsia. To obliterate this distinction it is necessary to raise the culture and technical education of the workers and peasants to the level of the intelligentsia.

The main means of solving this problem is technical progress and the attendant change in the nature of labour itself. Technological progress, the introduction of new complex and highly efficient machines, automation and complete electrification of production, the use of atomic energy and the wide application of the achievements of chemistry and other sciences demand not only special technical skills from the workers, but also an advanced general education and knowledge of the fundamentals of science. Technical progress is indissolubly bound up with the general cultural and technical advance of the workers and peasants. It is primarily in the process of *labour,* the main sphere of human activity, that an all-round developed individual will be moulded.

The system of public education also plays its part in eliminating the distinctions between mental and physical labour. This system is developing and improving, and establishing still closer ties with productive labour in order to enhance the education of the rising generation and the training of specialists for all the branches of the economy. The Soviet Union is broadening the network of correspondence and evening higher and secondary specialised educational institutions, general education schools, various schools of innovators, courses for agronomists and livestock specialists, and schools for farm-machinery operators so that an ever increasing number of workers and peasants will be able to raise their professional qualifications and cultural standards.

When communism is built there will no longer be any essential distinctions between mental and manual labour. Both the narrow, specialised mental labour and the purely manual labour will disappear in communist society. A qualitatively new type of labour will arise in which the physical and mental activity of the members of communist society, people of all-round development, will be harmoniously blended.

CHAPTER V

Historical Forms of Social Communities

We know that in addition to the mode of production, basis and super-structure a socio-economic formation includes definite historical communities of people—gens, tribe, nationality and nation. Let us examine these communities.

1. Gens, Tribe, Nationality, Nation

Gens and Tribe

A *gens* is a historical community of people who are united by blood relationships and certain economic ties, and who jointly protect common interests and combat the elements. The economic basis of a gens was collective ownership and use of the means of production. Its members worked together and together consumed the means of livelihood they produced. A gens was headed by a council made up of all the adult men and women who elected or removed the leaders—elders and military commanders.

In the initial stage of the development of the gens its members were those whose descent was reckoned through the mother (matriarchate). Later when the labour of men became socially more important, particularly with the spread of stockbreeding and tilling, the matriarchate was replaced by patriarchate. The father tried to leave the family property to his heirs and the gens' property gradually became separated from collective, clan property.

Several gentes would unite into a tribe characterised not only by a common ancestry, but also a common language and territory.

The gens and tribe existed under the primitive system and played a tremendous role in the development of society: people settled almost throughout the planet and laid the foundation for mankind's material and spiritual culture.

With the development of production and the rise of a class society and the state, blood relationships gradually fell apart and the gens and tribe gave way to a new historical community of people—the nationality. But the survivals of the tribal system persist for a long time and in some Asian and African countries they have remained to this day as a result of the imperialist colonial policy.

72

Nationality

As an historical community of people *nationality* is more typical of the slave-owning and feudal systems. Unlike the gens it is not based on consanguinity, but above all on common territory, language and culture. Nationalities emerged mainly as a result of the union of kindred tribes.

The common territory and community of language and culture typical of a nationality rested on a definite material foundation—natural, primarily agricultural economy with no social division of labour worth mentioning, peasant crafts and, later, manufacturing. Yet a nationality was not a sufficiently durable community of people because under the slave-owning system and feudalism the development of country-wide economic ties, without which close, stable connections between people could not emerge, was impossible. There were, of course, exchange of commodities and markets in the slave-owning society and under feudalism, but they were merely of local importance and were incapable of overcoming economic and political disunity.

Some nationalities that emerged in the slave-owning system and in a number of countries under feudalism have remained under capitalism and socialism but they have acquired specific capitalist or socialist features.

Nation

The disunity characteristic of feudal society disappears in the course of capitalist development and a single national market is formed as a result of which nationalities turn into *nations*. "Nations," wrote Lenin, "are an inevitable product, an inevitable form, in the bourgeois epoch of social development."*

A nation, like a nationality, has such features as common territory, language and culture. But as distinct from nationality it is a durable community of people and, as Lenin noted, it owes its durability to "profound economic factors".**

Community of economic life is a key feature of a nation. It is the economy, economic links that unite people living on common territory and having a common language into a single whole, into a nation. Economic and political development fosters a common psychology which is manifested in the historical traditions of a nation and in its distinctive culture and mode of life.

---

* V.I. Lenin, "Karl Marx", *Collected Works,* Vol. 21, p. 72.
** V.I. Lenin, "The Right of Nations to Self-Determination", *Collected Works,* Vol. 20, p. 397.

Nations are not *races*. Racial distinctions are certain external biological traits such as the colour of skin, the shape of the eyes, and others. On the basis of these distinctions humanity has been divided into three basic races: white, yellow and black.

Imperialist ideologists claim that the economic, political and cultural level of one or another people, or the position of a person in society depend on racial traits. They talk a lot about the ascendancy of the white race which, they say, has been assigned by nature itself to dominate the "coloured" races. But historical experience and scientific data prove that people of all races have equal abilities. As regards the backwardness of some peoples which do not belong to the white race, it is not due to the colour of their skin or hair, as bourgeois ideologists assert, but to the centuries of colonial oppression by the white exploiters. Now that they have cast off the imperialist yoke, the peoples of the former colonies and dependencies are successfully developing their economy and culture. Particularly rapid progress is being made by the socialist-oriented countries.

2. Nations and National Relations in Capitalist Society

Although the working class and other sections of working people make up the overwhelming majority of a nation in capitalist society, it is the bourgeoisie that plays the dominating role in it. All the means of production, state power and the mass media are in its hands. That is why bourgeois economy, politics and ideology in the main determine the image of a nation in capitalist society. The domination of economically and militarily more powerful nations over the weaker ones is consistent with the laws of development of bourgeois nations. This accounts for the fact that the development of nations under capitalism is inseverably connected with the intensification of the liberation struggle of the oppressed peoples. The *national question*, i.e., the question of the ways and means of the liberation of the oppressed nations, abolition of national oppression and the establishment of equal relations between nations is particularly acute under capitalism and is one of the main issues of social progress.

The content of the national question is not the same at various stages of capitalist development. In the rise of capitalist society this question did not, as a rule, transcend the limits of *individual* states. It was Russia, Austria-Hungary and some other multinational states, where some nations oppressed others, that were the main arena of the national liberation struggle. There the national question was in essence a question of national minorities, of their struggle for liberation and the right to establish their own statehood and economy, and foster their own culture.

National relations changed with the advent of the epoch of imperialism. The world split into a handful of dominating nations—the more advanced capitalist countries—and the majority of colonial and dependent nations and countries. Lenin regarded the division of nations into those that oppressed and those that were oppressed as "basic, significant and inevitable under imperialism".* The colonial system of imperialism came into being. Having entered the imperialist stage, capitalism, which at the dawn of its history helped the peoples to throw off the feudal and clerical yoke, turned into the greatest oppressor of nations and mercilessly suppressed the independence of peoples. Thus, the content of the national question changed and became much broader. It ceased to be an internal matter of a state and turned into an *international* issue bearing on the future of hundreds of millions of people.

Under imperialism the national question is no longer a question of national minorities within the boundaries of one state, but a *national-colonial question*. Above all it is a question of the people's struggle against the colonial rule, of their liberation and development along the road of progress.

Noting the importance of the national question, Marx, Engels and Lenin did not regard it, however, as the fundamental question of the revolutionary movement. They always subordinated it to what is the most important in Marxism—the teaching of the dictatorship of the proletariat—and viewed it from the standpoint of the interests of the international proletarian movement, the struggle for peace, socialism and social progress. They proceeded from the assumption that the national question as a whole could not be solved under capitalism, but only under the rule of proletariat, in a socialist society.

Lenin discovered two contrasting trends in the development of national relations under capitalism. One of them is manifested in the awakening to national life and in national movements, in the struggle against all national oppression and in the rise of national states. The other is expressed in the development of relations between different nations, in the destruction of national barriers, and in the formation of a single economy, of a world market. The first trend is predominant in the epoch of rising capitalism, the other, in the epoch of imperialism.

---

* V.I. Lenin, "Social Revolution and the Right of Nations to Self-Determination", *Collected Works*, Vol. 22, p. 147.

Both trends are consistent with social development and are progressive in terms of their inner historical meaning. But under capitalism they assume ugly forms that are incompatible with their objectively progressive content. Imperialism creates giant international banks and trusts and an all-embracing world economy, and increasingly unites, internationalises society's economic, political and cultural life. But this drawing together, "rapprochement" of nations under the domination of capitalist monopolies can take place only through violence, colonial plunder and the oppression of peoples by others that are more advanced and powerful. Under imperialism whole nations, big and small, and vast continents fell prey to the colonial expansion of a handful of imperialist predators who used the most brutal methods to crush all the efforts of the oppressed peoples to liberate themselves. It follows that the trend of the nations to draw together, to unite under capitalism directly contradicts the trend towards national independence and the formation of national states.

The above trends in the development of national relations are reflected in bourgeois ideology and policy and manifest themselves in the form of *nationalism*. Being intolerant of all manifestations of bourgeois nationalism, Marxism-Leninism at the same time draws a line between the nationalism of the dominating nations (Great Power chauvinism and racialism) and the nationalism of the oppressed nations. The ideology of Great Power chauvinism and racialism which justifies the domination of one nation over another is absolutely reactionary and is unconditionally rejected by the working class. On the other hand, the nationalism of the oppressed nations contains the progressive tendency of fighting for independence, against imperialism, and is therefore supported by the proletariat. "The bourgeois nationalism of *any* oppressed nation," Lenin wrote, "has a general democratic content that is directed *against* oppression and it is this content that we *unconditionally* support."* Such, for instance, is the nationalism of some Asian and African countries today. This nationalism owes its progressive nature to the struggle against imperialism and colonialism, against feudal reaction and backwardness, a struggle which awakens the self-awareness of the people, of millions of peasants in the first place.

It should not be overlooked that the progressive trend in the nationalism of the oppressed nations cannot be permanent. It is transitory because the historically progressive role of the national bourgeoisie in the national liberation movement is also transitory. Hence, when it supports the liberation

* V.I. Lenin, "The Right of Nations to Self-Determination", *Collected Works*, Vol. 20, p. 412.

struggle of the oppressed peoples, the party of the working class strives to rid the working people of the influence of nationalism, for bourgeois nationalism is incompatible with proletarian internationalism. By disclosing the decisive role played by the class struggle in any social movement, including the national movement, and appealing for the unity of the proletariat of all countries, a Marxist party overcomes the ideology of bourgeois nationalism and asserts *proletarian internationalism* in the consciousness of the working people.

The Collapse of Colonialism—a
Distinctive Feature of
the Contemporary Epoch

In the face of inhuman exploitation by the imperialist predators the peoples of the colonies and dependent countries launched a liberation struggle against colonial oppression, for freedom and national independence.

The new correlation of forces on the international scene after the Second World War, the triumph of socialist revolutions in a number of European and Asian countries, and the emergence of the world socialist system created especially favourable conditions for the successful national liberation struggle of the peoples. Imperialism suppressed the national independence and freedom of the majority of the peoples and put the fetters of brutal colonial slavery on them, but the *rise of socialism marks the advent of the era of emancipation of the oppressed peoples.* A powerful wave of national liberation revolutions is sweeping away the colonial system and undermining the foundations of imperialism. Young sovereign states have arisen, or are arising, in one-time colonies or semi-colonies.

There have been victorious revolutions in Ethiopia, Afghanistan, Nicaragua, and Iran. The Republic of Zimbabwe has come into being and the liberation struggle in Namibia and South Africa is growing. During the 1970s the colonial empires virtually ceased to exist.

Radical changes have taken place in Asia and Africa. Latin America, where U.S. imperialists held undivided sway for decades, is rising for the struggle against the domination of foreign monopolies. Heroic Cuba, where a people's revolution was accomplished, has become a beacon for the peoples of Latin America in their just struggle for national freedom and social progress. It will not be long now before colonialism, that infamous phenomenon in human history, will be wiped out for ever. The complete collapse of colonialism is inevitable. The downfall of the system of colonial slavery under the onslaught of the national liberation movement ranks second in historical importance to the formation of the world system of socialism. The significance of the disintegration of the colonial system of imperialism lies in the fact that it awakens fresh hundreds of millions of people to the task of moulding their own history. The peoples of the sovereign states that have emerged on the ruins of the colonial empires are now building a new life and actively participating in world politics, and are one of the mighty revolutionary forces that are destroying capitalism.

The peoples that have rent the yoke of colonialism are destined to play a great role in averting another world war and preserving and strengthening peace. Together with the peoples of the socialist countries they comprise two-thirds of humanity which is a great force that can compel the imperialist aggressors to retreat.

Many complex tasks confront the peoples of the liberated countries. The most important of them is to choose the path of further development. The bourgeoisie endeavours to direct the development of the nations along the capitalist road and thus preserve private ownership and exploitation. As regards the masses, the working people, they are beginning to realise that *socialism is the only road that leads to freedom and happiness.*

It is up to the peoples themselves to choose their path of development. Today, in view of the growth of revolutionary forces in the world and the existence of the world socialist system upon whose support and assistance the newly-free peoples can rely, they can advance towards socialism *bypassing capitalism,* by taking the path of socialist orientation. In order to accomplish this great social leap they have to struggle and to work with the utmost dedication, building up material (modern production) and social (working class and its party) conditions for the socialist transformation of society.

3. Socialism and Nations

Solution of the National Question in the USSR

Capitalist society, which is based on private ownership and exploitation and foments discord and hostility between peoples, cannot solve the national question. Only socialism, which eliminates exploitation and class antagonisms, puts an end to national discord and ensures the true flourishing, mutual trust and rapprochement of the peoples. "In proportion as the exploitation of one individual by another is put an end to, the exploitation of one nation by another will also be put an end to."*

The socialist revolution in the USSR sundered the chains of national oppression, vanquished the age-old enmity between peoples and paved the way for their all-round cooperation and rapprochement. It granted the people the right to decide their own future and develop national statehood, economy and culture.

The Communist Party and the socialist state attached special importance to the national question from the moment the Soviet Republic was founded. Already on November 15, 1917 the Soviet Government adopted the Declaration of Rights of the Peoples of Russia which solemnly proclaimed the equality and sovereignty of all its peoples, and their unlimited right to self-determination up to and including secession and the formation of independent states. It repealed all national privileges and restrictions and guaranteed the free development of national minorities and ethnic groups.

The adoption of this declaration signified the abolition of national oppression and the establishment of political and juridical equality of the numerous nations and nationalities inhabiting the country. It also laid a firm foundation for the voluntary alliance of all nations and nationalities into a single state. This unification was completed in the formation, on December 30, 1922, of the Union of Soviet Socialist Republics, the world's first multinational state based on national equality and voluntary accession. The establishment of the USSR enhanced the economic and military might and the political status of the Soviet republics and created conditions for the further drawing together of the peoples and for their joint struggle for socialism. Needless to say, the emancipation of nations could not be confined solely to the abolition of national oppression and ensurance of their political and juridical equality. The main thing was that the Soviet socialist state successfully accomplished the difficult task of surmounting the age-old economic and cultural backwardness inherited by the new society from tsarist Russia. It not only granted the formerly oppressed nations the right to free development, but helped them to overcome their backwardness and raise their national economy and culture to great heights.

Having rehabilitated the economy that the imperialist First World War and the Civil War had left in ruin, the Communist Party and the Soviet Government immediately launched the industrialisation of the national republics. Thanks to the concern of the Party and the state and the disinter-

---

* Karl Marx and Frederick Engels, "Manifesto of the Communist Party", in: Karl Marx, Frederick Engels, *Collected Works,* Vol. 6, p. 503.

ested assistance of other nations, the Russians in the first place, the formerly backward republics set up new branches of industry which developed at an unprecedented rate. It should be noted that these rates of growth were considerably higher than the rate of industrial development in the USSR as a whole. For instance, while gross industrial output in the whole of the USSR in 1940 was 11.7 times greater than in 1913, the figures for Kirghizia and Tajikistan were 153 and 277 respectively. Ferrous and non-ferrous metal, automobile, electrotechnical and other new branches of industry appeared in the national republics.

Agriculture — in these republics also changed beyond recognition: it is now collective and highly mechanised.

The development of the productive forces in the Soviet republics stimulated the growth of skilled national personnel and a numerous intelligentsia. Cultural backwardness was surmounted. *The peoples of the Soviet Union accomplished not only a most profound revolution in the economy, but also the greatest cultural revolution.*

There is universal literacy in all the Soviet republics, which have numerous schools, institutions of higher learning and research and cultural establishments. They have a flowering culture which is socialist in content and national in form. In terms of cultural growth the Soviet national republics have greatly outstripped not only the capitalist countries of the East but also many industrialised capitalist countries in the West.

Thus, as a result of the victory of socialism in the USSR, Russia's former national borderlands that were tsarism's economically and culturally backward raw materials appendages, became advanced sovereign socialist republics with a highly developed industry and productive agriculture, with their own working class and a numerous intelligentsia.

Bourgeois nations became qualitatively new *socialist nations*. Numerous nationalities also consolidated socialist nations on the new socio-economic basis. Many of them bypassed the capitalist stage and with the help of other, more developed peoples, reached the level of the advanced nations.

The development of nations in the USSR does not take place through the strengthening of national barriers and cultivation of national narrow-mindedness and egoism as is the case in capitalist society, but through the drawing together of nations, their fraternal mutual assistance and friendship. The rapid and all-round development of each nation, on the one hand, and the increasing rapprochement of socialist nations on the basis of proletarian internationalism, on the other, are the two interconnected progressive *tendencies* in the national relations under socialism. As a result, a new, formerly unknown historical community, the Soviet people which is based on the solid alliance of the working class, the peasantry and the intelligentsia; the friendship of all the big and small nations of our country, has come into being. This community arose on the basis of public ownership of the means of production, uniformity of economic, socio-political and cultural life, Marxist-Leninist ideology and interests and communist ideals of the working class.

Relations of fraternal cooperation and mutual assistance between peoples, relations that had never before existed in the world took shape in the USSR on the basis of the complete domination of socialist relations of production. The lasting friendship of the peoples of the USSR which became a permanent factor of Soviet reality as a result of the victory of socialism in the country has turned into a mighty motive force of socialist society and a major source of its indestructibility and strength. The full and consistent solution of the most complicated national question inherited by the USSR from the old system vividly attests to the triumph of the ideas of Marxism-Leninism, of proletarian internationalism.

Judging by the great progress of the Soviet nations and nationalities it is clear that only socialist revolution creates conditions for the complete elimination of national oppression, for the voluntary union of free and equal peoples in a single state, for the true flourishing and rapprochement of nations. Today the states of the world socialist system draw upon the Soviet Union's experience as they try to solve the national question at home and within the framework of the socialist community of nations as a whole. This invaluable experience is also of great importance for the peoples of the young sovereign national states that had cast off the colonial yoke, and for peoples who are fighting against colonialism. For them the successes of the peoples of the USSR are a source of inspiration and strength in their difficult fight against imperialism. In the present of the socialist nations they see their own future.

Developed socialism and the building of communist society are a new stage in the development of national relations in the USSR which is characterised by the further drawing together of nations and the achievement of full unity, and not only legal but actual equality.

The creation of the material and technical base of communism stimulates the further all-round development of the economy of the Union republics, improves the division of labour between them and promotes the expansion of the existing and establishment of new economic links. Each of them contributes to the common cause of augmenting the growth of the country's productive forces and fostering closer economic unity of the socialist nations.

The successes in socialist construction, the obliteration of class distinctions solidify the social homogeneity of nations and stimulate the development of common features in their culture, morality and mode of life. All this enhances their mutual trust and friendship. The spiritual unity of nations is strengthening. There is an all-round flourishing of the socialist culture of the peoples of the USSR and mutual enrichment and rapprochement of the national cultures.

Taking the interests of the Soviet state into consideration, the Party will continue undeviatingly to pursue the Leninist line of strengthening the Union of Soviet Socialist Republics. It will also take into account the specific conditions of development of each of the Soviet republics as it works consistently to promote the further burgeoning and rapprochement of all socialist nations.

The further drawing together of nations in the course of socialist construction is an objective process, and the Party is both against spurring it on artificially and against any attempts to hold it up, to create obstacles in its way under any pretext and to deliberately consolidate national isolation. The Party resolutely counters all manifestations and survivals of nationalism and chauvinism, and opposes tendencies towards national seclusion and exclusiveness, the idealisation of the past and concealment of social contradictions in the history of peoples, and obsolete customs and morals.

The drawing together of nations will eventually lead to their merger. But the merger of nations and the obliteration of distinctions between them is a much longer process than the obliteration of distinctions between classes. Class distinctions will disappear with the victory of communism, but national distinctions, particularly in language, will persist for a considerable time.

4. The family

Family as a Social Group

Another important social group is the *family.* It is a very complex and specific group of people whose natural and social functions, the latter being predominant, closely intertwine. The natural (physiological) function finds its expression in the relations between sexes, and in the birth of children. But all this acquires a social and, in a class society, a class content. Relations between men and women, parents and children, population growth, etc., depend on social, above all economic, relations, on the mode of production.

The family is the product of marriage, a more or less stable, intimate union between man and woman which in a certain way governs their relations and ensures the birth of children. This union presupposes mutual attraction, common interests and spiritual affinity of husband and wife.

What is the family's social content and what are its social functions?

In a class society the family has three social functions: First, regulation of the *relations between sexes* on the basis of society's dominant economic and political system and specific legal and ethical norms.

Second, the *reproduction and education of posterity,* of people who are social beings capable of working, or, in other words, the *reproduction of labour power.*

Third, *housekeeping* and *servicing* its members.

It follows that the family performs very important social functions and is closely connected with the entire system of social relations. Possessing as it does a certain amount of property (household goods and chattels at least), a family in a class society is an elementary economic cell which, while enjoying relative independence, is a part of the system of society's economic relations. Since it is subject to legal and ethical norms, the family is also part of the system of ideological, spiritual relations.

Types of Families

A family is an *historical* category. It changed and developed as the mode of production and social relations changed and developed. In the primitive herd, which preceded the tribal system, relations between sexes were of a haphazard nature and consequently no family existed. As a social phenomenon the family appeared in the primitive society. At first, at the *matriarchate* stage it had a *group character* when all the women of a gens were the possible wives of all the men of another gens. Children did not know their fathers. They belonged to the maternal family consisting of a group of the mother's nearest relatives. Gradually a *paired family* appeared within the group marriage. At first it was a chance, temporary cohabitation of individual pairs, and then it developed into a more or less lasting one. The fragile paired family which had no household of its own was replaced by a more durable *monogamic* family which arose following the transition from the matriarchate to the patriarchate. The husband and father became the head of the family, and his wife and children lived with him under one roof. The family acquired property which the children inherited from the father together with his name.

With the rise of the class antagonistic society the development of the family became closely connected with the development of private ownership and relations of exploitation. At first it was a slave-owning family; then it was succeeded by a feudal and capitalist family depending on changing socio-economic systems.

In the slave-owning and feudal societies a slave or a peasant could have a family only with the consent of, or at the discretion of, his master. As regards slaves they were often enough forbidden to have families. Under feudalism relations in a family acquired a clearly expressed class nature: marriages between people belonging to different estates were not permitted. A typical feature of a slave-owning or feudal family was the unlimited authority of its head over his wife, children and property, and the debased and oppressed status of the woman.

The rule of the family head and the unequal status of the woman are preserved in the capitalist family in spite of the proclaimed freedom of marriage-family relations. The role played by material considerations was never greater than it is in a bourgeois family whose main aim and purpose is accumulation of wealth and its inheritance by descendants.

Another family which exists in capitalist society is that of a working man. Here marital relations usually rest on love, respect and cooperation of husband and wife. But this family, too, experiences the demoralising influence of capital. Capitalism deprives many low-paid workers, not to mention the unemployed, of a chance of marrying. A woman under capitalism carries a double burden: she is forced to work for the capitalist and usually for a lower wage than a man, and also to do the lion's share of the work involved in housekeeping and bringing up children. The woman's unequal status is determined by law and consecrated by bourgeois morality and religion.

The Socialist Family

By doing away with private ownership and exploitation socialism puts an end to all oppression and inequality, including the inequality of women. It makes for a harmonious family, frees it from the influence of the principles of private ownership and creates conditions for the family and marriage to rest on the love, friendship and cooperation of husband and wife. Here the woman has equal rights with man. She has every opportunity to work and get paid on a par with men, be active in public life and in administering society, and to develop intellectually. Women in the USSR comprise a considerable part of industrial workers, collective farmers and the intelligentsia; they make up the majority of school teachers, medical workers and the personnel of the services. Hundreds of women are deputies of the highest organ of state power, the USSR Supreme Soviet. Women participate in all spheres of social activity thanks to the concern for women, mothers and children on the part of socialist society, which has built numerous nurseries, kindergartens, boarding schools, public catering establishments and set up an extensive service industry. All this helps to strengthen the family and introduce socialist, truly humane principles into family relations. A socialist family is a qualitatively new type of family created by the very essence of socialism, by socialist social relations.

It should be borne in mind that survivals of the past, primarily a certain inequality of women in family, in everyday life, continue to exist under socialism. In a socialist society a family has its household economy and most of the tasks involved are performed by women who as a rule also play a great part in bringing up children. Survivals of the old, feudal attitude to women (early marriages, bride-money, etc.) still exist in some national republics. However the last vestiges of the inequality of women are gradually disappearing.

Society will assume the main burden of the provision of everyday services and child upbringing. A family will gradually cease to be an economic cell, but it will continue to perform the functions of regulating relations between sexes, of reproduction and of bringing up children.

CHAPTER VI

The State

No question has been more confused by bourgeois sociologists than that of the state, Lenin pointed out, because no other question is as vital to the interests of the ruling classes. Bourgeois ideologists picture the state as some kind of supernatural force given to man by providence since time immemorial. It supposedly has no class character and is merely an innocuous "instrument of order", an "arbiter" called upon to resolve disputes which may arise between people regardless of their class affiliation. Such a "theory" of the state serves to justify the privileges of the bourgeoisie and the existence of exploitation and capitalism.

Marxism-Leninism alone has scientifically explained the origin of the state, its essence and the role it plays in society's life.

1. The Origin and Essence of the State

The State as a Product of Society's Historical Development

In contrast to bourgeois ideologists, Marxism has demonstrated that the state is not something introduced into society from the outside, but is a product of society's internal development. The state was brought into being by changes in material production. The succession of one mode of production by another causes a change in the state system.

The state has not always existed. Primitive society which had no prlvate property and no classes had no state either. Naturally, there were certain social functions, but they were performed by men chosen by all of society which had the right to dismiss these people at any time and to appoint others. In those distant times relations between people were regulated by public opinion.

The further development of the productive forces, as we have already observed, led to the disintegration of primitive society. Private property appeared, accompanied by classes—slaves and slave-owners. It became necessary to protect private property, the rule and security of its owners, and this brought the state into being. The birth of the state and its further development were accompanied by a fierce class struggle.

The state is a product of *class* society. It arose with the appearance of classes and it will vanish, wither away with the disappearance of classes. But this will happen only under communism.

The Essence of the State

In an antagonistic class society the *state* is a political instrument, "a machine for maintaining the rule of one class over another".* The class dominating economically, i.e., possessing the means of production, acquires in the state a powerful instrument for the subjection of the oppressed and exploited. The state has a clearly defined class character. Being the principal component of the superstructure founded on the economic basis of society, the state takes every measure to strengthen and protect this basis.

What are the features of a state?

The main feature of a state is the existence of *public* (social) authority representing the interests of the class which dominates economically and not of the entire population. This authority rests on armed force—the army and the police.

In primitive society all the people were armed. But in a society divided into hostile classes, the armed forces are in the hands of the ruling class and are used to suppress the people, to subordinate them to a handful of exploiters. Representative bodies (parliaments), the huge bureaucratic administrative machine with a whole army of officials, intelligence agencies, the courts, procurator's offices and prisons—all are used for the same purpose. All of them combined make up the political authority of the exploiting state.

As class contradictions deepen and the class struggle intensifies, the state machine expands. This process is particularly intensive in contemporary capitalist society where the state machine and the armed forces have grown to an unprecedented size. The maintenance of this colossal state machine and the armed forces is a heavy burden for the people, especially today when imperialist circles are engaged in the arms race.

While in primitive society people settled in consanguineous groups, in a state the population is grouped *territorially,* i.e., in districts, counties, states, regions, etc. Territorial settlement is a result of the development of production, the increasing division of labour and the growth of trade and commodity exchange.

* V.I. Lenin, "The State", *Collected Works,* Vol. 29, p. 478.

2. The State in an Exploiting Society

Functions of Exploiting States

The state of any exploiting society (slave-owning, feudal, or capitalist) is designed to protect the interests of the ruling class both within the country, in relations with other classes, and outside, in relations with other states. There are therefore two main trends or functions in the activities of a state: internal and external. The internal function is the main one and it determines all the foreign affairs of a state.

Let us examine these functions.

The *internal* function of an exploiting state is to suppress the working people, to subordinate them to the small group of oppressors. This reflects the class nature of the state and is expressed in its internal policy, the struggle against the oppressed classes. Economic compulsion alone, which the exploiters can apply owing to their monopoly over the means of production, is not enough to win this struggle. They need a special political machine of coercion, the exploiting state.

The first exploiting state was the slave-owning state. It was succeeded by the feudal state, which in turn was superseded by the capitalist state. In spite of certain differences, all the three had one task in common: to keep the people in check and to crush any attempt of the working people to emancipate themselves from exploitation.

The slave-owning state used armed force to put down the slaves who rose against their masters. The feudal state forcibly bound the peasants to the landlord's estate and cruelly punished those who refused to toil for the landlord. The numerous peasant uprisings ended in blood baths. The capitalist state, although it likes to parade in democratic garb, is also a machine for the subjection of the working people. Its real purpose is to protect private capitalist property, maintain wage-slavery and crush the revolutionary movement of the proletariat.

The *external* function of the exploiting state is to seize foreign territories or defend its own land from attack. This is reflected in its relations with other states and is expressed in its foreign policy. Foreign policy stems from home policy and is a continuation of the latter. The reactionary, predatory foreign policy of contemporary imperialism is a natural supplement to its home policy of suppressing the working class and all other progressive forces.

Types of State and Forms of Rule

States differ according to the class they serve and the economic basis on which they arose. Four *types* of state are known in history: slave-owning, feudal, capitalist and socialist. In contrast to the first three, which defend the interests of the exploiters, the socialist state is a state of a *new type,* a genuine state of the *people.*

Each type of state has its intrinsic *form of government,* i.e., order, organisation of rule by the dominant class. The form of government depends on the concrete historical conditions in each country, on the balance of the class forces and external conditions. However diverse the forms of government, however much they may change, the type of state, its class nature, remains unaltered within the framework of the given economic system.

Lenin noted that a slave-owning society had different forms of government: a monarchy—the rule of one man, the emperor, the monarch; a republic—elective rule; aristocracy—the rule of a relatively small minority; democracy—the rule of the majority. In spite of these differences, the state in the slave-owning era, Lenin said, was a state of the slave-owners.

Feudal society presented a similar picture. A monarchy was the most widespread form of government in the feudal state, but at times it also appeared in other forms, for example, a republic. Whatever the form, the feudal state served as an instrument for suppressing the serfs and the artisans.

Diversity of form is also true of the bourgeois state. Most frequently this state appears as a republic (the United States, France, Italy and other countries). Under capitalism the monarchic form seldom exists and the rule of the monarch is in one way or another restricted by the constitution (Britain and Belgium). In the imperialist era the bourgeoisie also makes use of fascist dictatorship (Hitler Germany, Franco Spain, and so on). The unlimited power of the bourgeoisie is exercised in any form of the bourgeois state.

With society's development the types and forms of the state changed.

Reactionary Nature
of the Contemporary Bourgeois State

Bourgeois ideologists and politicians are fond of talking about the progressive role of the bourgeois state. They claim that only this state has brought the people full freedom, that it is the highest type of democracy, genuine democracy. Today reformists are particularly vociferous in this respect. They portray the bourgeois state as a force standing above classes, equally restraining both labour and capital. The capitalist state, in their opinion, has ceased to be the organ of only one class, the capitalist class, and now serves all classes in society. There is, however, no evidence to support the statements of the reformists about the progressive, democratic nature of the contemporary bourgeois state.

At the dawn of capitalism the bourgeois state did in fact possess some progressive features: it helped to introduce and develop capitalist production relations, which were more advanced than feudal relations. Even in its heyday, however, the bourgeois state was not a democracy for all, but only for the select, for the bourgeoisie. The democracy of capitalist society, Lenin wrote, is democracy for the negligible minority, for the rich.

The bourgeois state, whatever its form, is dictatorship of the capitalists, a machine for suppressing the working class and all working people which always employs coercion against its class enemies in varying degrees and forms. With the advent of imperialism the bourgeois state directly turns towards reaction and assumes the inglorious historical role of defending the economic basis of imperialism which long ago became a brake on historical progress.

Imperialism is reaction along all lines, Lenin wrote, in state policy first of all. "Both in foreign policy and in home policy imperialism equally strives towards violation of democracy, for reaction. In this sense imperialism is indisputably the 'negation' of democracy in general, of all democracy."*

State-monopoly capitalism becomes widespread under imperialism. It combines the power of the monopolies with the power of the state into a single machine for enriching the monopolies, crushing the proletarian movement and the national liberation struggle, attempting to save the capitalist system and unleashing aggressive wars. The state becomes a committee for administering the affairs of the monopoly elite. In the interests of the latter the state constantly interferes in the process of capitalist production, applies various regulating measures and takes over individual branches of the economy in order to ensure the maximum profits to the monopolies.

The reactionary nature of the home and foreign policies pursued by the contemporary bourgeois state cannot be concealed either by oratory about freedom, democracy, human rights, references to bourgeois constitutions or declarations about the civilising mission of capitalism. The constitutions

---

** V.I. Lenin, "A Caricature of Marxism and Imperialist Economism", *Collected Works*, Vol. 23, p. 43.

of many imperialist states are not wanting in articles proclaiming all sorts of freedoms and rights for all citizens— universal suffrage, free elections, freedom of speech and of the press, and so on and so forth. In reality these freedoms often remain a dead letter for the overwhelming majority of citizens, for the working people. Only the bourgeoisie, which controls all the instruments of economic and political domination, enjoys them to the full.

The "free" world of capitalism has millions of unemployed; in other words, bourgeois rule is unable to ensure the right to work for everyone.

However much the capitalists and their lackeys boast about the capitalist paradise, capitalism remains a system of oppression of an overwhelming majority of people by a handful of exploiters, a society where lack of rights, poverty and unemployment are the lot of millions of working people. The essence of "freedom" in the imperialist world is freedom to exploit the working class and all working people not only at home but also in other countries.

Under imperialism, the financial oligarchy increasingly resorts to the most reactionary methods of government—to outright terrorist dictatorship, to fascism; it relies on the army and the police as a last resort to protect it from the people's wrath and hold up its inevitable doom.

Mankind has not forgotten the horrors of the fascist regimes of Hitler, Mussolini and their allies in Europe, the horrors of the Second World War unleashed by fascism. Dangerous signs of fascism, however, have reappeared in some capitalist countries. Complete subordination of the state to the giant monopolies, militarisation of the economy, expansion of the state machine, the frenzied drive against the working-class and the communist movement, persecution of peace supporters and members of other progressive organisations, racial discrimination and restriction of democratic freedoms—this is the content of the domestic policy pursued by contemporary imperialist states.

The foreign policy of contemporary imperialist states is also reactionary. Posing as champions of "liberation" of the colonial peoples, the imperialists are actually waging a vicious struggle against the national liberation movement and are imposing in new forms the very same colonialism which is so hated by the peoples. In order to gain control over countries which have formally won their independence, the imperialists inveigle them into their aggressive blocs, make use of economic "aid" to less developed countries and other means. They support reactionary regimes, engage in the arms race and have surrounded the Soviet Union and other socialist countries with a ring of military bases.

The imperialist states, characteristically enough, pursue their reactionary domestic and foreign policies under the flag of struggle against the "communist menace" from the Soviet Union and the other socialist countries, despite the fact that neither the Soviet Union nor any other socialist country threatens anyone. On the contrary, the states of the socialist system are the most consistent fighters for peace throughout the world, for peaceful coexistence with the capitalist countries.

The working class cannot be indifferent to the form of bourgeois state that exists in its country. Despite the restricted nature of bourgeois democracy, it affords the working class more favourable conditions than open dictatorship for waging a successful struggle against the bourgeoisie, for the dictatorship of the proletariat and for socialism. That is why the working class in the capitalist countries, heading all the progressive forces, persistently combats the onslaught of the reactionaries, and fights for democracy and curtailing monopoly rule.

3. Dictatorship of the Proletariat

The proletariat has the great historical mission of destroying capitalism and building a classless communist society. Yet this new society does not grow out of capitalism directly and at once. Between capitalism and socialism "lies the period of the revolutionary transformation of the one into the other. Corresponding to this is also a political transition period in which the state can be nothing but *the revolutionary dictatorship of the proletariat.*"*

*Dictatorship of the Proletariat
as a Qualitatively New Type of State*

The dictatorship of the proletariat arises as a result of the successful socialist revolution and thorough demolition of the bourgeois state machine. It is a qualitatively new type of state and differs radically from the previous states in regard to its class nature, the forms of state organisation and the role it is destined to play.

All the preceding types of state were tools of the exploiting classes used for the subjection of the working people and designed to reinforce the system of exploitation and to perpetuate the division of society into oppressors and oppressed. The dictatorship of the proletariat, however, is the rule of the working class which, together with all other working people, destroys

---

* Karl Marx, "Critique of the Gotha Programme", in: Karl Marx and Frederick Engels, *Selected Works* in three volumes, Volume Three, p. 26.

capitalism and builds a new society, a society without antagonistic classes and exploitation.

"If we translate the Latin, scientific, historico-philosophical term 'dictatorship of the proletariat' into simpler language," Lenin wrote, "it means just the following:

"Only a definite class, namely, the urban workers and the factory, industrial workers in general, is able to lead the whole mass of the working and exploited people in the struggle to throw off the yoke of capital, in actually carrying it out, in the struggle to maintain and consolidate the victory, in the work of creating the new, socialist social system, in the entire struggle for the complete abolition of classes."*

The theory of the dictatorship of the proletariat is the *crux* of Marxism. Only dictatorship, the undivided power of the proletariat, enables the proletariat to put an end to capitalism and build socialism. It is only natural, therefore, that the question of the dictatorship of the proletariat has always been, and remains, the pivot of the ideological struggle of Marxism- Leninism against reformism and revisionism. Lenin called the dictatorship of the proletariat the touchstone for testing the real understanding and recognition of Marxism. To be a Marxist it is not enough merely to recognise the struggle of classes, he said. You can be a Marxist only if you extend recognition of the class struggle to recognition of the dictatorship of the proletariat.

Lenin implacably fought against the reformist leaders of the Second International and revisionists who denied the need for the dictatorship of the proletariat. He tirelessly proved that the dictatorship of the proletariat is the only means for building socialism. And history has fully corroborated him. It is due to the dictatorship of the proletaliat that socialism scored complete and final victory in the Soviet Union, and that other countries are successfully advancing along the socialist road.

Present-day revisionists, however, continue to deny the need for the dictatorship of the proletariat, although they do so in more refined ways than their predecessors. Unable to ignore the existence of the dictatorship of the proletariat in the countries of the socialist system, they do not regard it as a universal, natural form of transition from capitalism to socialism, but as a national form applicable only to economically backward countries like the pre-revolutionary Russia. They assert that dictatorship of the proletariat is applicable only in economically backward countries, with a low level of development of the productive forces and almost no forms of political

---

* V.I. Lenin, "A Great Beginning", *Collected Works,* Vol. 29, p. 420.

democracy. As regards the industrialised countries, there, in the opinion of the revisionists, the transition to socialism is effected through "pure democracy", meaning bourgeois democracy.

The views of the reformists and revisionists run counter to history, which convincingly shows that it is impossible to build socialism without the dictatorship of the proletariat. In the course of socialist construction, the dictatorship of the proletariat solves a number of major problems by performing specific *functions*—the main aspects of its activity. We shall now examine these functions.

Functions of the
Dictatorship of the Proletariat

The state of the dictatorship of the proletariat is a state which exists in the period of the transition from capitalism to socialism. This period is characterised by a multistructural economy and the bitter class struggle between the proletariat and the bourgeoisie. The crucial task facing the proletariat at that time is to break down the resistance of the bourgeoisie, and together with all the working people to build socialism. This task determines the functions of the proletarian state.

One of the main *domestic* functions of the proletarian state in the transition period is the *function of suppressing the exploiting classes*, the bourgeoisie in the first place. Deprived of its political domination the bourgeoisie in any country cannot reconcile itself to its defeat and the loss of power and privileges, and therefore viciously resists the victorious proletariat.

The dictatorship of the proletariat is necessary for overcoming the resistance of the bourgeoisie, for defeating it in fierce class battles. "The dictatorship of the proletariat," Lenin wrote, "means a most determined and most ruthless war waged by the new class against a *more powerful enemy*, the bourgeoisie, whose resistance is increased *tenfold* by its overthrow...."[*]

The suppression of the exploiters is a compulsory task of the proletarian state whatever its form, but this can be done in various forms depending on historical conditions.

The suppression of the bourgeoisie, however, is not an aim in itself for the proletariat. Its main aim is to *build socialism*, to create a new, socialist economy. What makes this task so difficult is that the socialist revolution begins when there are no ready-made economic forms of socialism. It is

---

[*] V.I. Lenin, " 'Left-Wing' Communism—An Infantile Disorder", *Collected Works*, Vol. 31, p. 23-24.

the task of the dictatorship of the proletariat, of the proletarian state, to organise the economic life of society, to build up a new type of economy superior to capitalism, the economy of socialism. "The dictatorship of the proletariat," Lenin wrote, "is not only the use of force against the exploiters, and not even mainly the use of force.... The proletariat represents and creates a higher type of social organisation of labour compared with capitalism. This is what is important, this is the source of the strength and the guarantee that the final triumph of communism is inevitable."*

The activities of the state in building up socialist economy and guiding all economic affairs in the country is the main *economic and organisational function* of the state of the dictatorship of the proletariat. The task of the proletarian state in fulfilling this function is to secure socialism's economic victory over capitalism and attain a higher level of the social organisation of labour than under capitalism. Once it has nationalised the basic means of production the proletarian state immediately takes over command positions in the economy and organises its planned, science-based management. Under the guidance of the Marxist party the state carries out the socialist industrialisation of the country and collectivisation of agriculture and, on the basis of the continuous development and improvement of production, raises the material wellbeing of the people. As socialism progresses the economic and organisational function of the state gains in scope and with the victory of socialism embraces literally all branches of the national economy.

Yet socialist construction is not confined to the establishment of a socialist economy. It is inconceivable without a steadfast growth of the awareness and culture of the people, and the obliteration of the survivals of the past in their consciousness. It is only natural, therefore, that the education of the working people, particularly the semi-proletarian strata and the peasantry, in the spirit of socialism, the promotion of their general education and professional and cultural level is one of the key tasks of the proletarian state. It is all the more important to solve this problem because the exploiters for centuries enslaved the working people and in every way suppressed their striving for culture and knowledge. The proletarian state guides the cultural revolution which is an important element of the socialist revolution. The role played by the state in promoting cultural development and the education of the working people finds its expression in its *cultural and educational function*.

---

* V.I. Lenin, "A Great Beginning", *Collected Works*, Vol. 29, p. 419.

In the sphere of *foreign policy* the activity of the proletarian state is characterised by the *function of the struggle for peace* between the peoples, and the *function of the country's defence* against imperialist aggression. As it persistently works for peace the state of the dictatorship of the proletariat constantly strengthens the country's defence and its armed forces.

A New Type of Democracy

Bourgeois ideologists and their reformist hangers-on shout from the rooftops about "universal democracy", "democracy for all", which allegedly exists in the capitalist world. They hold up this "pure" bourgeois democracy in contrast to the dictatorship of the proletariat which is supposed to be a bureaucratic, undemocratic rule.

In reality the very opposite is the case. The much-vaunted bourgeois democracy, as we have already seen, is merely a screen for the omnipotence of the moneybags and for the actual lack of rights of the working people. The aim of bourgeois democracy is to perpetuate the capitalist system, the exploitation of the millions of working people by the negligible minority of the rich.

Only the proletarian state is truly democratic. The dictatorship of the proletariat is a qualitatively new *type of democracy*. This, as Lenin wrote, is democracy for the overwhelming majority of the people and the exclusion of the exploiters and oppressors from this democracy. In the process of its development it increasingly turns into socialist democracy *of the whole people*.

The qualitatively new type of democracy under the dictatorship of the proletariat stems from its very nature, its aims and purposes. Only in a firm alliance with all the working people and with the democratic forces, only with the support of the masses can the proletariat break down the resistance of the exploiting classes, retain power, build socialism and in this way bring the people a life of happiness. That is why the *alliance of the working class* and the non-proletarian sections of town and country, above all the *peasants,* constitutes the basis, the *supreme principle* of the dictatorship of the proletariat, the fullest and all-round expression of the genuine democracy of the proletarian state.

The alliance of the working class with the working people of town and country is founded on the community of their basic political and economic interests, on the common desire to abolish exploitation and build socialism. Only socialism is capable of emancipating the workers from capitalist wage-slavery and the peasants and other non-proletarian working sections from ruin and poverty. It was in joint struggle against exploitation, for the new, socialist system that the alliance of the working class with all the working people and democratic forces arose and is developing. It is the source of the might of the proletariat.

The proletariat, however, Lenin noted, does not need just an alliance with semi-proletarian strata, but one in which it plays the leading role. The peasants and the other petty bourgeoisie are inconsistent. They are, at the same time, both working people and small owners and they often vacillate between the proletariat and the bourgeoisie. Only the proletariat, the most advanced, consistently revolutionary and organised class, headed by the Marxist party, is capable of overcoming their vacillation, wresting them away from the bourgeoisie and leading them along the socialist road.

A primary distinction of proletarian democracy is that it not only proclaims the rights of the working people, but also provides the conditions for the people to exercise them. Under the dictatorship of the proletariat the working people possess not formal rights, as in a bourgeois state, but they actually govern the country and directly, or through their representatives, manage its entire economic, political and cultural life.

The proletarian state guarantees the exercise of democratic rights by providing the corresponding material facilities. The working people own all the means of production, and this enables them to manage the country's economy and to exercise their right to work. Schools, universities, scientific and cultural institutions, health and holiday homes give them the opportunity to exercise their rights to education and to rest and leisure. The working people have at their disposal printshops, stocks of paper, radio stations, the best buildings, etc., and this enables them to enjoy freedom of the press, speech, assembly, freedom of organisation, etc.

The working people actively take part in the political life of the country, in state affairs, through their wide participation in the Soviets or other state bodies, in numerous committees and commissions set up by the Soviets and also through their own social organisations. In a word, proletarian democracy, as Lenin said, is a million times more democratic than any bourgeois democracy.

Various Forms of the Dictatorship of the Proletariat

The transition from capitalism to socialism can take place through the dictatorship of the proletariat. However, being the content of the transition period, the dictatorship of the proletariat can assume different forms in different countries. "All nations will arrive at socialism—this is inevitable," Lenin stated, "but all will do so in not exactly the same way, each will contribute something of its own to some form of democracy, to some variety of the dictatorship of the proletariat, to the varying rate of socialist transformations in the different aspects of social life."*

The form of the dictatorship of the proletariat depends above all on the concrete historical conditions in a country, i.e., on the level of its economic development, the balance of class forces and the acuteness of the class struggle, the national and historical traditions of the people and on the international situation.

In 1917, the revolutionary action of Russia's working class brought into being such a form of the dictatorship of the proletariat as the *Soviets of Workers', Peasants' and Soldiers' Deputies*. In a number of other European and Asian countries another form of the dictatorship of the proletariat, *People's Democracy,* came into being.

What are the differences between such forms of the dictatorship of the Proletariat as People's Democracy and the Soviets?

Firstly, a People's Democracy has a multi-party system, i.e., it allows the existence of a number of parties standing for socialist construction and recognising the leading role of the Communist Party. For instance, a multi-party system has taken shape in Bulgaria, the German Democratic Republic, Poland and Czechoslovakia. The Soviet Union, however, has a one-party system, because the petty-bourgeois parties of Russia, the Left Socialist-Revolutionaries, for instance, refused to cooperate with the Communists and sided with the counter-revolutionaries.

Secondly, a People's Democracy has a people's (national) front—a mass organisation which unites the most diverse sections of the people for the purpose of building socialism. The people's front is a specific organisational form of the alliance between the working class, the peasants, intellectuals and also the petty bourgeoisie and part of the middle bourgeoisie, in which working class and its party play the leading role.

Thirdly, in the European People's Democracies the parliamentary forms and traditions were used in the fight against capitalism and for socialism. In autocratic Russia the parliamentary system was not widely developed and had no established parliamentary traditions. People's Democracy, as a form of the dictatorship of the proletariat, reflects the specific development of the socialist revolution in conditions when imperialism is weakened and the correlation of forces in the world changes in favour of socialism. It is

---

* V.I. Lenin, "A Caricature of Marxism and Imperialist Economism", *Collected Works*, Vol. 23, pp. 69-70.

also dependent upon the historical and national peculiarities of the countries which have embarked on the socialist road of development.

History has so far produced two forms of the dictatorship of the proletariat, the Soviets and the People's Democracy. But other forms of the dictatorship of the proletariat could also arise. In those cases, too, the leading role of the working class and its Marxist party is absolutely essential. "The transition from capitalism to communism is certainly bound to yield a tremendous abundance and variety of political forms, but the essence will inevitably be the same: *the dictatorship of the proletariat,"* Lenin pointed out.

*The Leading Role of the Marxist Party
in the Dictatorship of the Proletariat*

The Marxist party, as the advanced, politically aware and organised detachment of the working class, is that leading force which brings about the overthrow of the political rule of the bourgeoisie and the establishment of the dictatorship of the proletariat. It is difficult to seize power, but it is much more difficult to retain it, to finally defeat the overthrown bourgeoisie, and it is incredibly harder (a thousand times more difficult, as Lenin put it) to eradicate the private-property instincts of millions upon millions of peasants and other small owners, to wrest them away from the bourgeoisie and turn them into politically aware builders of socialism. The working class can accomplish these extremely hard tasks and build socialism and then communism only if it maintains the strictest organisation and discipline and is confident that it has chosen the right road. Only the *Marxist party* can organise the proletariat, maintain iron discipline in its ranks, educate the working class, protect it from petty-bourgeois influence, direct its political activities and, through it, influence all the working people. That is why the successful building of socialism is inconceivable "without a party of iron that has been tempered in the struggle, a party enjoying the confidence of all honest people in the class in question, a party capable of watching and influencing the mood of the masses...".**

After the victory of the socialist revolution, the Marxist-Leninist party becomes the party of the ruling class. This places special responsibility upon it and immeasurably enhances its role as the leader of the working class. Utilising its knowledge of the objective laws of social development

*V.I. Lenin, "The State and Revolution", *Collected Works*, Vol. 25, p. 413.
**V.I. Lenin, " 'Left-Wing' Communism—An Infantile Disorder", *Collected Works*, Vol. 31, p. 44.

and summing up and drawing upon the revolutionary experience of the people, the party directs all the economic, political and cultural activities of the proletarian state. It maps out a single political line in all spheres of the country's life and works to ensure the application of this line.

Under the dictatorship of the proletariat the unity of the Marxist party is more important than ever before. Only if there is unity of will and action among all its members will the party be able to lead society, uphold and consolidate the rule of the working class and organise the building of socialism and communism. The Communist Party of the Soviet Union and the Communist and Workers' parties in all the other countries which embarked on the road to socialism are irreconcilably opposed to any factionalists and splitters who seek to undermine the unity of the party.

The Marxist party exercises its leading role through the system of state bodies and numerous social organisations— trade unions, co-operatives, all kinds of youth, artistic and other organisations. The party unites the efforts of these organisations and directs them towards one goal; it does not substitute for state and other bodies, but stimulates their initiative to the utmost and strives for the broadest democracy in their activities. Through a network of state and social organisations the party is connected with millions of working people, teaches and educates them and learns from them. The party solves all the principal problems of socialist construction together with the people, with the entire proletarian state in which the people are widely represented.

The Marxist party constantly works to strengthen the proletarian state, to develop democracy, to enlist more and more people in administering the country. The broad ties which are formed between the party and the people in the course of the struggle against imperialism develop in the period of the dictatorship of the proletariat into a *solid unity of the party and the people*. This is the source of the strength of the Marxist party and an earnest of the success of its great cause.

4. The Socialist State

The consolidation of the economic basis occasioned changes in the socialist superstructure, particularly in the state and its functions. Let us consider these changes.

The State of the Whole People

With the completion of socialist construction the state of the dictatorship of the proletariat turns into a *state of the whole people*—the political organisation of the whole people in which the leading role is played by the working class and its vanguard, the Communist party.

The main tasks of this state, says the Constitution of the USSR, are "to lay the material and technical foundation of communism, to perfect socialist social relations and transform them into communist relations, to mould the citizen of communist society, to raise the people's living and cultural standards, to safeguard the country's security, and to further the consolidation of peace and development of international co-operation".*

A distinctive feature of the state of the whole people is that it does not have to perform the function of suppressing the exploiting classes because they have ceased to exist as a result of the victory of socialism. This, however, does not mean that the working class has completely withdrawn from the class struggle: it wages its class struggle in close unity with the cooperated peasantry and the intelligentsia *against international imperialism and bourgeois and petty-bourgeois ideology.* Furthermore, relying on the support of all working people, on their consciousness and organisation, it takes recourse to necessary measures of *coercion* with regard to persons who violate the laws, standards and principles of socialist society.

Dictatorship of the proletariat and the state of the whole people are not qualitatively different types of state. In point of fact they are stages in the development of a socialist-type state. The state of the whole people continues the cause of the dictatorship of the proletariat and organises the building of socialist society. Its social basis is the working class, the collective-farm peasantry and the intelligentsia, with the working class—the most advanced, organised and conscious force of socialist society—playing the leading role. The state of the whole people raises to a new height that which was the main content of proletarian dictatorship—proletarian, socialist democracy. It preserves and develops the basic functions of the dictatorship of the proletariat, with the exception, as we have noted, of the function of suppressing exploiters.

It follows that the socialist state invariably safeguards people's rights and freedoms and socialist law. The state is particularly concerned with safeguarding socialist property, the economic foundation of socialism. *The protection of socialist property and of the rights and freedoms of Soviet citizens, and the maintenance of socialist law and order* are important functions of the socialist state. Having emerged at the initial stage of its existence, these functions became fully developed under socialism.

---

* *Constitution (Fundamental Law) of the Union of Soviet Socialist Republics,* pp. 14-15.

With the victory of socialism in the USSR the socialist state began to exercise its main functions, that of managing the economy and promoting culture and education, to the full.

Owing to rapid economic growth, the *managerial function* became much more complex and multiform. In the transition period from capitalism to socialism this function of the state was designed to ensure the economic victory of the socialist forces over the capitalist forces in the country, whereas with the building of socialism its purpose is to build the material and technical base of communism, transform socialist relations into communist relations and further improve the wellbeing of the people. The state is coming to play an increasing role in controlling the measure of labour and the measure of consumption.

With the completion of socialist construction a major change took place in the Soviet state's *cultural and educational function*, for the higher the consciousness and culture of the people, the faster the transition to communism. The moulding of a new man unweighted by survivals of the past, a profoundly educated, conscious toiler for whom work for the benefit of the country is not an obligation but a vital requirement, the cause of his life.

The *foreign policy function* of the Soviet state broadens in the period of the gradual transition from socialism to communism in view of the serious changes in the international situatiton. The *strengthening and development of the fraternal cooperation with the socialist countries*—such is the new function of the Soviet state which it has to perform in view of the rise of the world socialist system. Another new function is to *support the struggle of the peoples for liberation from colonial and neocolonial oppression*. The Soviet state has preserved and broadened its function of *working for universal peace and maintaining normal relations with all countries*.

At the same time the state strengthens the country's defensive capacity in every way because, as long as imperialism which is pregnant with the threat of aggressive wars exists, a socialist country cannot feel itself ensured against attack. Protection of the socialist homeland, *the organisation of its reliable defence and security* and the strengthening of the Soviet Armed Forces are important functions of the socialist state. At the same time the Soviet Union regards as its internationalist duty to ensure together with other socialist countries the security and defence of the entire socialist system.

The Further Development of Socialist Democracy

The solution of the tasks involved in the improvement of socialism is inconceivable without the further development of democracy and active participation of all people in socialist construction.

The CPSU and the Soviet Government are consistently strengthening the Leninist norms of party life and government activity and further broadening Soviet democracy. The Leninist principle of democratic centralism which ensures the proper combination of centralised leadership with the maximum encouragement of local initiative, the extension of the rights of the Union republics, local organs of government and economic executives, has been given all-round development.

Legislation in the fields of law, the administrative and territorial structure and in other important fields of economic, state and cultural development has been invested in the Union republics. The Soviets of People's Deputies play an increasing role in communist construction. By their very nature the Soviets have been and continue to be not only state organisations but also public organisations, and, in view of the increasing and direct participation of the people in their activity, are becoming even more so as society advances towards communism. For example, more than 30 million activists take part in the work of the standing commissions, non-staff departments, people's voluntary inspections, groups of non-staff instructors, etc., which have been set up by the Executive Committees of the Soviets.

A law was adopted in the USSR on the status of a deputy which precisely defines the rights and duties of deputies, and the duties of state and public bodies with respect to them. Laws on village, settlement, district and city Soviets were also passed. They enhanced the role of these bodies in directing economic, social and cultural development on territories under their administration.

On October 7, 1977, the new *Constitution (Fundamental Law) of the Union of Soviet Socialist Republics—the law of life of developed socialism—* was adopted. It gives a full picture of mature socialism, its economic and political system, social structure and spiritual development and its foreign policy, and shows the great gains of socialist democracy, the extensive rights and freedoms of the citizens and their duties, the national-state structure of the USSR, the system of the organs of power and administration, and other important principles of statehood.

The development of democracy in a socialist society finds its expression in *the growth of the role played in it by mass public organisations of the working people—* the trade unions, the Leninist Young Communist League (YCL), cooperatives, and cultural and educational societies. Public organisations have always been faithful assistants of the Communist party and the Soviet Government, channels of their policy, and in the course of communist construction their functions in the solution of important matters of state will continue to grow.

The *trade unions* play an increasing role in the spheres of economic and cultural development. They are a school of communist education, a school of economic management.

The trade unions directly further the exercise of democracy in production, the basic sphere in which man's creative efforts are applied. Their main task is to protect the rights and interests of the working people and actively deal with everyday social questions. The trade unions are wholly dedicated to the working man's interests and, therefore, they are concerned with boosting production, strengthening labour discipline and promoting labour productivity.

A major role in communist construction and the communist education of young people is played by *YCL* members. The task now facing the YCL is to further increase the participation of young people in economic and cultural development, in the country's political affairs, to cultivate in young men and women a high level of ideological integrity and devotion to the Party's cause, love for their socialist homeland, preparedness to protect it, a sense of fraternal friendship for the people of other socialist countries, and internationalist solidarity with all the exploited and the oppressed.

The importance of the *co-operatives* (collective farms, consumer and other co-operative organisations) is growing, and creative unions, scientific, technical, cultural and educational, sports and other societies and organisations are broadening their activities.

The role played by work collectives is also increasing. As the USSR Constitution notes they take part in considering and deciding state and public affairs, in planning production and social development, in training and placement of personnel, in examining and deciding matters pertaining to the management of enterprises and offices, the improvement of working and living conditions, the administration of funds allocated for expanding production and for social and cultural purposes and material incentives. Work collectives promote socialist emulation, the spread of advanced methods of work, and the strengthening of labour discipline, educate their members in the spirit of communist morality, promote their political awareness, culture and professional skill.

Development of socialist democracy directly depends on the consolidation of the state, the increased organisation of society and the consolidation of socialist law and order and discipline. With this aim in view the Party helps to improve Soviet legislation, the work of the militia, the procurator's offices, courts and judiciary bodies.

The CPSU's Growing Role

The Communist Party of the Soviet Union, states the USSR Constitution, is the leading and guiding force of Soviet society, and the nucleus of its state system and of all state and public organisations. The CPSU exists for the people and serves the people. Armed with Marxism-Leninism the Communist Party determines the general perspectives of the development of society and the course of the home and foreign policy of the USSR, directs the great constructive work of the Soviet people and imparts a planned, systematic and theoretically grounded character to this work. All Party organisations function within the framework of the Constitution of the USSR. By means of a system of state and public organisations the Party brings its ideas to the masses in the form of specific, concrete tasks   and directs the efforts of each collective, of all Soviet people toward solutions

The role played by the Communist Party increases in the course of further development. This is due to the growing scope and complexity of the tasks, the rise in the creative activity of the masses, the further development of socialist democracy, the mounting importance of scientific theory and the need to improve the communist education of the working people.

The Party is a living, developing organism which steadfastly augments its ranks and takes care that the working class occupies the leading position in its social composition. It improves the forms and methods of its work, bringing them into conformity with life and the needs of communist construction. Its main task is to formulate the general perspective of social development, a correct political line, and to organise the people for the job of translating it into reality. The Party directs the communist education of people, supervises the selection and placement of cadres and verifies the execution of its own and the state's decisions.

In its life and work the Party abides by Leninist principles and norms which have been checked, confirmed and enriched in the course of decades of historical experience. The most important of these principles, a tested weapon and the Party's greatest political asset is *collective leadership*. Only on the basis of the Leninist principle of collective leadership is it possible correctly to analyse the situation, soberly and objectively appraise successes and bring to light and cope with shortcomings in good time. Complacency and admiration of its own successes are alien to the Party. It critically assesses its activities, strives to concentrate on shortcomings and unresolved questions, and to continuously improve the organisation, forms and methods of its work.

The Party's tested organisational instrument for ensuring the victory of communism are Party Rules which impose high demands on each member:

a Communist has to exemplify a conscientious attitude to labour, lofty moral fibre, tact and consideration for people, dedication to the party and the people, intolerance of shortcomings; money-grubbing and parasitism. They also envisage the further development of inner-party democracy, and the enhancement of the role of the party's local organs and primary organisations. The party regards it as its duty to consult the people on all key issues of home and foreign policy, and to draw the non-party masses into its activity.

5. The Withering Away of the State

The fact that it is necessary to strengthen and develop the socialist state does not mean that it will exist for ever. *As socialist statehood develops, it will gradually become communist self-government of the people* that will embrace the Soviets, trade unions, cooperatives, and other mass organisations of the people.

Needless to say, public functions similar to those performed by the state today in the sphere of economic and cultural management will be preserved under communism. They will be modified and perfected as society develops. But their character and the ways in which they are carried out will be different from those under socialism. The state bodies lose their political character as society moves towards communism. With time they will merge with society and become organs of public self-government through which *all members of society* will participate in economic and cultural management. The state will wither away.

It would be incorrect, however, to imagine that the withering away of the state and the transformation of state administration into public self-government under communism will take place suddenly and all at once. The withering away of the state is a long gradual process covering an entire historical epoch. For a certain period elements of state administration and public self-government will coexist and intertwine, and the need for the state will disappear only when society becomes fully mature for self-government, i.e., under developed communism. "The state will be able to wither away completely when society adopts the rule: 'From each according to his ability, to each according to his needs', i.e., when people have become so accustomed to observing the fundamental rules of social intercourse and when their labour has become so productive that they will voluntarily work *according to their ability*."*

* V.I. Lenin, "The State and Revolution", *Collected Works*, Vol. 25, p. 474.

The *internal condition* for the withering away of the state is the building of developed communist society. But there have to be *external conditions* too for the state to wither away, namely the victory and consolidation of socialism on the international scene. When speaking about the withering away of the state it is necessary to take the international situation into account. If communism triumphs in one or another country or a group of countries, but armed imperialist predators continue to exist in the world, then the communist society will definitely retain the state function of defending the country. This function will become obsolete only when the threat of an attack by reactionary imperialist forces disappears for ever.

CHAPTER VII

The Social Revolution

We have seen in the preceding chapter what the state is, how it arose and what types of states are known in history. The following questions now arise: Why is one type of state replaced by another?

Why do social orders change?

Why is one ruling class replaced by another?

How do social orders and types of state change?

The Marxist-Leninist theory of the social revolution answers these questions.

1. The Social Revolution—a Law of Development of an Antagonistic Class Society

The Essence, Causes and Significance of the Social Revolution

A *social revolution* is a deep-going upheaval in the political, economic amd ideological life of society. It is a revolution that brings about the succession of ruling classes and types of states, abolishes old relations of production, introduces new ones and radically changes social views and institutions.

A *social* revolution does not take place by accident but is a *natural* product of the material conditions of society's life at definite stages of its development, of its internal contradictions. Pointing to the causes of the social revolution, Marx, in his preface to *A Contribution to the Critique of the Political Economy* wrote that at a certain stage of their development, the productive forces of society come in conflict with the existing relations of production within which they have hitherto been at work. From forms of development of the productive forces these already obsolete relations turn into their fetters. Then begins an epoch of social revolution.

The conflict between the new productive forces and the old relations of production is the objective economic foundation of the social revolution. We have ascertained earlier that relations of production cannot indefinitely lag behind the development of the productive forces. Sooner or later they must conform to them. And they are brought into conformity by a social revolution.

A conflict in the sphere of production is always expressed in a conflict of class interests. The reactionary class, the vehicle of old relations of production, is opposed by the progressive class, the vehicle of new relations of production. Hence the irreconcilable struggle of the progressive class against the reactionary class, of which the social revolution is the highest expression and the consummation.

The old, reactionary class never gives up its rule voluntarily. It uses the full power of the state to preserve the old production relations. To abolish the old production relations and introduce new ones, therefore, the progressive class must gain political power. In other words, whether the new relations of production win or not ultimately depends on whether the revolutionary class gains state power. Therefore *state power is the basic question of any revolution.*

Social revolutions are of tremendous importance in the life of society. It is only through radical, revolutionary changes that the old, reactionary social system can be abolished and a new, progressive system introduced. Only social revolutions resolve economic and class contradictions which matured in the long period of preceding social development. Only revolution helps to remove obstacles to economic, political and cultural progress (obsolete production relations and their reactionary vehicle, the old classes). The creative energies of the people are awakened in time of social revolution, and millions upon millions of people are drawn into active social life, as a result of which the process of social development is greatly accelerated. For this reason Marx called revolutions the locomotives of history.

A Revolutionary Situation.
The Role of the Subjective Factor in a Revolution

A revolution is not made "to order" or at someone's will. Definite historical conditions, objective and subjective prerequisites, are necessary for a revolution.

The sum of objective conditions needed for a revolution is called a *revolutionary situation.* Lenin regarded the following as signs of a revolutionary situation:

1. On the one hand, the impossibility for the ruling classes to live and rule in the old way, the so-called crisis "from above", and, on the other, the unrest of the oppressed classes which do not want to live in the old way, the

crisis "from below". "Revolution is impossible without a nation-wide crisis (affecting both the exploited and the exploiters),"* Lenin wrote.

2. Extreme aggravation of the poverty and suffering of the oppressed classes.

3. A considerable increase in the activity of the people. While in ordinary times the masses are relatively calm, in conditions of crisis the situation itself impels them to take independent revolutionary action.

Not every revolutionary situation, however, leads to a revolution. There was a revolutionary situation in Russia from 1859 to 1861, but no revolution occurred. A revolutionary situation, the maturity of the objective factor, merely creates the possibility for a victorious revolution. But to turn this possibility into reality the *subjective factor*, too, must be ripe, i.e., the revolutionary class must be ready and able to undertake revolutionary mass action which is sufficiently strong to overturn (or undermine) the old government which, as Lenin wrote, will never "fall" until it is "pushed". A victorious socialist revolution is possible only if the working class is organised and politically aware, if it has reliable allies and the revolution is led by an experienced, battle-seasoned Marxist party.

The Nature and Driving Forces of a Revolution

Social revolutions differ in nature and driving forces. The *nature* of a revolution depends on the class which comes to power and the relations of production introduced as a result of it. For example, a revolution in the course of which the rule of the feudal lords is replaced by the rule of the bourgeoisie and correspondingly new capitalist relations of production are established instead of feudal relations, bears the nature of a bourgeois revolution.

The *driving forces* of a revolution are the social classes which make the revolution and fight against the reactionary classes for the triumph of new relations of production. One of the classes making the revolution is the leader and it is followed by all the other classes and social groups taking part in the revolution.

What the driving forces of a revolution are and what class is the leader depends both on the nature of the revolution and the historical conditions in which it takes place. In the bourgeois revolutions which took place in the West when capitalism was on the ascent (from the 17th to the first half of the 19th century) the driving forces were the peasants and the artisans,

---

* V.I. Lenin, " 'Left-Wing' Communism—An Infantile Disorder", *Collected Works*, Vol. 31, p. 85.

while the leader was the bourgeoisie which led all the other fighters against feudalism.

Bourgeois revolutions in the era of imperialism often acquire a strongly pronounced democratic nature (the revolution of 1905-07 and the February revolution of 1917 in Russia). The widest sections of the people take part in them, they put forward their own demands, pursue an independent line and exert a tremendous influence on the course of the revolution. The imperialist bourgeoisie acts as a reactionary class in these revolutions. It is afraid of the full victory of the revolution, fears wide democratisation, because the fuller the freedom and the wider the democracy, the more favourable the conditions for the struggle of the working class against its rule. The monopoly bourgeoisie seeks to end the revolution halfway by coming to terms with the landlords, with the old authority. That is why in the new conditions the monopoly bourgeoisie ceases to be the leader and the driving force of the revolution; in a number of countries it openly supports the counter-revolution. The proletariat and the peasants, with the proletariat as the leader, are the driving forces of bourgeois revolutions in the epoch of imperialism.

2. A Socialist Revolution

In order to get rid of exploitation and national oppression, unemployment and poverty, the proletariat has to destroy capitalism and establish socialist society. *This can be achieved only through a socialist revolution.*

Essence of the Socialist Revolution

A socialist revolution radically differs from all the preceding types of social revolution.

What is the difference?

Firstly, all previous revolutions did not aim to abolish exploitation, but merely modified its forms. A socialist revolution, however, *abolishes every exploitation for all time* and ushers in the era of construction of a classless society.

Secondly, previous revolutions did not have to create a new economy. They only brought political power into line with the new economic relations which arose within the old society. One of the principal tasks of a socialist revolution is *to create a new economy,* the economy of socialism which does not arise within the womb of capitalism.

Thirdly, no revolution is marked by such great *activity of the people* as a socialist revolution. In the course of it the proletariat rallies round itself the broad sections of the working people and the democratic forces to fight against capitalism and for socialism.

The working class is the decisive force of a socialist revolution. Headed by the Marxist party the proletariat, being the most advanced, revolutionary class, leads all the working people who are fighting against the old, capitalist society. It organises the attack on capitalism, which holds political sway, and establishes its own rule. Having seized political power, the working class continues to lead all the working people along the socialist road.

The main question of a socialist revolution is the *winning of political power by the proletariat* and its further development and consolidation. We know that the working class can discharge its mission—abolish capitalism and build a new society—only by creating its own proletarian state. The destruction of the bourgeois state machine and the building of a new, proletarian state are the principal tasks of a socialist revolution.

Inevitability of the Socialist Revolution in the Epoch of Imperalism

Reformists have always opposed the socialist revolution. They are particularly obstinate in their attempts to refute the Marxist-Leninist theory of the socialist revolution at the present time, when mankind's movement from capitalism to socialism is the main feature of history. In order to prevent this law-governed process at all costs, preserve capitalism and divert the working class from revolutionary struggle, the reformists claim that in present-day conditions there is no need for a socialist revolution, that the possibility has arisen for the evolution from capitalism to socialism through reforms. Contemporary capitalism, they maintain, has ceased to be the capitalism of which Marx wrote in *Capital;* it has become "people's capitalism", a society without exploiters and exploited. The bourgeois state, too, has changed: they claim that it has lost its class nature and has become a "welfare state" capable of bringing about socialism by reforms within the framework of the existing political system.

The views of the reformists who deny the need for a socialist revolution have been taken up by contemporary revisionists. The growth of state-monopoly planning and regulation of economy in a number of capitalist countries is their main argument attesting to the conversion of contemporary capitalism into socialism. They regard the mounting state-monopoly tendencies in capitalist countries as graphic proof that mankind has entered the era of socialism.

Revisionists do not even toy with the idea of destroying the cornerstone of capitalism, private property; they refuse to see that state-monopoly capitalism which they extol, far from abolishing, only concentrates property in the hands of the capitalist state, and even if it has any plans they are designed solely to sweat the working people even more "systematically". They deny the leading role of the proletariat in the revolution and the need for a proletarian state.

Facts show that no "people's capitalism", capitalism without exploiters, no "welfare state" exists under imperialism, nor could there be any. Imperialism possesses an extremely reactionary nature expressed in greater exploitation of the working class, a frenzied drive on the standard of living and democratic rights of the working people, the arms race and preparations for another world war. All this inevitably deepens the antagonism between the working class and all the working people, on the one hand, and the bourgeoisie, on the other, which is expressed in sharper class struggles, wider popular movements against imperialism, for an improvement of their standard of living, for peace, democracy and socialism. This struggle naturally leads to the victorious socialist revolution, to the abolition of capitalism and to the victory of socialism.

The socialist revolution is inevitable in the epoch of imperialism. Only the proletarian revolution is capable of removing capitalist production relations, the formidable obstacle to the development of the modern productive forces, to mankind's progress, and of meeting the most pressing requirements of historical development. And although imperialism is still strong enough and superprofits enable it to bribe the upper crust of the working class, although bourgeois ideologists and their revisionist aides so far succeed in addling the minds of part of the working people, capitalism is historically doomed.

Lenin's Theory of the Socialist Revolution

The founders of scientific communism, Marx and Engels, proved that the doom of capitalism and the victory of socialism were inevitable. They exposed the antagonism between the bourgeoisie and the proletariat and reached the conclusion that the further development of this antagonism unfailingly led to socialist revolution.

They, however, lived at a time when capitalism was on the upgrade and developed more or less evenly. Proceeding from this, they held that the proletarian revolution could be victorious simultaneously in all, or in a majority of the advanced countries, because at that time any attempt to establish socialism in one country would have been crushed by the combined efforts of all the capitalists.

At the turn of the century, when capitalism entered its final stage, imperialism, and the conditions for the socialist revolution substantially altered, Lenin advanced a new theory of the revolution corresponding to the epoch of imperialism.

In his book *Two Tactics of Social-Democracy in the Democratic Revolution,* Lenin elaborated the important question of *the bourgeois-democratic revolution growing into the socialist revolution.* Analysing the specific features of the revolutionary movement of the working class in the new historical conditions, above all the specific features of the 1905-07 revolution in Russia, he came to the conclusion that only the proletariat, which is directly interested in taking the revolution right to the end, could and should be the leader of the bourgeois-democratic revolution in the period of imperialism. In the course of the revolution the proletariat first carries out democratic changes and then, as Lenin pointed out, proceeds at once from the democratic to the socialist revolution.

Lenin's brilliant discovery of the *possibility of the socialist revolution being victorious first in one country or several countries,* is the most important element in his theory of the revolution. To substantiate this discovery he referred to the fact that the development of capitalist countries under imperialism is uneven, spasmodic. Some countries, which formerly fell behind, overtake and outstrip the economically advanced countries. The balance of forces is upset, and conflicts and wars for the redivision of the world break out. As a result, the positions of world capitalism are weakened and the possibility arises of breaking the chain of imperialism at its weakest link. "The development of capitalism proceeds extremely unevenly in different countries," Lenin wrote. "It cannot be otherwise under commodity production. From this it follows irrefutably that socialism cannot achieve victory simultaneously *in all* countries. It will achieve victory first in one or several countries, while the others will for some time remain bourgeois or pre-bourgeois."*

Lenin's theory of the socialist revolution has tremendous practical significance. It unshackles the revolutionary initiative of the working people and makes the working class of each country confident in the victory of

---

* V.I. Lenin, "The Military Programme of the Proletarian Revolution", *Collected Works,* Vol. 23, p. 79.

its great cause, in the inevitable doom of capitalism and the victory of socialism and communism.

3. The Triumph of Lenin's Theory of the Socialist Revolution in the Contemporary Era

Guided by Lenin's theory of the socialist revolution, Russia's working class, in alliance with the peasants and headed by the Bolshevik Party, abolished the rule of the landlords and capitalists, and took political power into its own hands. 7 November 1917 has gone down in history as the beginning of a new era in mankind's development—the era of the fall of capitalism and the triumph of the new, socialist society. "From now on," Lenin said on that historic day, "a new phase in the history of Russia begins, and this, the third Russian revolution, should in the end lead to the victory of socialism".*

His words were prophetic. The almost 70 years that have passed since that day have strikingly proved the correctness of the ideas of Marxism-Leninism and proletarian internationalism. Mankind saw the rise of a true socialist society whose very existence repudiates exploitation and all forms of social oppression. The building of developed socialism is the main result of the growth of Soviet society since the Great October Socialist Revolution.

This revolution gave a powerful impetus to the world revolutionary movement, contributed to the further disintegration of the capitalist system and deepened the general crisis of capitalism. It inaugurated the transition from capitalism to socialism.

After the Second World War a number of countries in Central and Southeast Europe and Asia fell away from the capitalist system. Capitalism ceased to be the only world socio-economic system. Two systems now exist in the world—moribund capitalism and the young and growing socialism.

The World Socialist System

The world socialist system is a social, economic and political community of free, sovereign peoples, having embarked on the socialist and communist path, and united by an identity or interests and goals, and the close

---

* V.I. Lenin, "Meeting of the Petrograd Soviet of Workers' and Soldiers' Deputies, October 25 (November 7), 1917", *Collected Works*, Vol. 26, p. 239.

bonds of international socialist solidarity. The states of this system occupy a large territory of Europe, Asia and Latin America. The socialist community is the most dynamic, economically stable and progressive force in the world. The CMEA member countries alone, which account for just slightly over 10 per cent of the earth's population, produce more than 33 per cent of world industrial output.

The world socialist system is a *qualitatively new type of economic and political relations between countries*. These relations are based on the identity of their economic and political interests and the single Marxist-Leninist ideology. Social ownership of the means of production is the economic foundation of the socialist system. Its political foundation is the rule of the people headed by the working class. Its ideological foundation is the theory of Marxism-Leninism. Socialist countries have one goal—the building of socialism and communism.

Full equality of states, big and small, non-interference in each other's domestic affairs, respect for national sovereignty and territorial integrity, fraternal economic assistance, close cooperation in the economic, political and cultural spheres—these are the basic principles underlying the relations between the socialist countries.

The forms of cooperation and mutual assistance between the socialist countries are very diverse. In the economic sphere they are expressed in the socialist economic integration, the coordination of national economic plans, specialisation and cooperation of production, all-round scientific and technical cooperation, etc. In the political sphere they consist in joint struggle against imperialist reaction, for peace, socialism, and social progress. In the sphere of culture they are manifested in ever wider and multifarious cultural cooperation between the socialist countries, resulting in greater mutual enrichment of their national cultures.

The establishment of a new type of relations and cooperation between socialist countries is a fairly complicated process, with its specific difficulties and problems. The reason is that these countries have different levels of economic and cultural development, different histories, traditions and customs. Moreover, as the peoples draw closer together they have to overcome the survivals of the past, and particularly of nationalism, in their consciousness. Hence the need to strengthen the unity of the socialist countries which multiplies the might of socialism and helps it to successfully counter the forces of imperialist reaction. The Communist Party of the Soviet Union makes every effort to promote the cohesion of the socialist community on the basis of Marxism-Leninism, and to enhance its might and influence; it broadens economic, scientific, technical and ideological cooperation and cultural links, and educates the Soviet people in the spirit of friendship and international solidarity with the peoples of the fraternal countries.

Transformation of the World Socialist System into a Decisive Factor of World Development

History has witnessed numerous clashes between different social systems which in the final count ended in the victory of the more progressive ones. And there can be no doubt that the present struggle between the two opposing systems—socialism and capitalism—will end in the complete victory of the socialist system. This firm belief rests on a scientific amalysis of the laws of social development, on the facts of life. There can be no better proof of the strength and vitality of socialism than such events of world-historic importance as the victory of the Great October Socialist Revolution and the consolidation of socialism in the USSR, and the development of the world socialist system. At the same time the aggravation of the general crisis of capitalism, the falling away of a number of countries from the capitalist system and the collapse of the colonial system of imperialism leave no doubt that the doom of capitalism is inevitable.

The world of socialism is expanding while the world of capitalism is shrinking. Socialism will inevitably replace capitalism everywhere. Mankind's transition from capitalism to socialism is the main content of our day and age. "Our epoch, whose main content is the transition from capitalism to socialism," states the CPSU Programme, "is an epoch of struggle between the two opposing social systems, an epoch of socialist and national liberation revolutions, of the breakdown of imperialism and the abolition of the colonial system, an epoch of the transition of more and more peoples to the socialist path, of the triumph of socialism and communism on a worldwide scale. The central factor of the present epoch is the international working class and its main creation, the world socialist system."*

The entire course of mankind's development in our epoch convincingly shows that the world system of socialism now stands in the centre of the socialist and of all progressive forces of the world in general. Being a beacon for mankind's progessive movement and exerting revolutionary influence on the course of world development, the world socialist system is at the same time a great material force embodying the immortal ideas of Marxism-Leninism, a force which bears the main burden of the struggle

* *Road to Communism,* p. 449.

against imperialism and the greater share of responsibility for the future of the world.

Above all the socialist system influences the course of world development by its economic growth whose high rates continuously augment its share in world industrial and agricultural production. The greater the socialist system's success in economic development and the bigger its economic and political potential, the more important is the role it plays in finding solutions to crucial international issues, the problem of war and peace in particular. Thanks to the strength of the forces of socialism and peace it is now possible not only to expose but also frequently to cut short the reactionary intrigues of the imperialists.

The world socialist system plays a tremendous role in modern history also due to its ever increasing influence on the struggle of the peoples of the non-socialist states. By force of example it revolutionises the minds of the working people in capitalist countries, inspiring them to fight against capitalism, and for peace and social progress, for the triumph of democracy and the victory of socialism. Today the peoples which are stirring to revolutionary action can rely on the support from the socialist system in their struggle against the export of counter-revolution by the world revolution. The socialist countries also assist them in the building of a new society.

The socialist countries are the most irreconcilable opponents of colonialism and staunch champions of national equality and state independence of the peoples. The world socialist system opposes colonial domination and gives every support to the struggle of the peoples for independence; it is a mighty factor of the further successes of the national liberation movement.

Peaceful Coexistence as a Form of Resolving Contradictions Between the Two Opposing Systems

A specific form of resolving contradictions between the world socialist and capitalist systems is *peaceful coexistence* of states with different social systems.

The principle of peaceful coexistence was formulated and substantiated by Lenin. He firmly believed that sooner or later socialism would triumph throughout the world, but maintained that this victory would not take place in all countries at one and the same time. Depending on the level of economic development, the acuteness of the class struggle, the correlation of forces between the proletariat and bourgeoisie and other conditions, some countries would arrive at socialism sooner than others. Proceeding from this premise, Lenin drew the conclusion that during a certain historical period when there would be both capitalist and socialist countries in the world, the *coexistence of socialist and capitalist countries is inevitable*. Lenin was a proponent of *peaceful* coexistence, and the CPSU and the Soviet Government firmly adhere to this principle in their foreign policy whose main aim is to ensure peaceful conditions for the building of communism in the USSR and the development of the world socialist system, and, together with all the peace-loving peoples, to save mankind from the horrors of a devastating world war.

Today when there are monstrous weapons of mass destruction and the means for delivering them to any point on the globe, when another world war would take a colossal toll of lives and cause terrible destruction, the problem of war and peace has become the most acute issue of our time. It has become a problem of life and death for hundreds of millions of people, a problem of the very existence of whole nations and states. That is why the peoples are against war and for peaceful coexistence.

Peaceful coexistence presupposes renunciation of war as a means of settling international disputes, and their solution by negotiation; equality, mutual understanding and trust between countries; consideration for each other's interests; non-interference in each other's domestic affairs and recognition of the right of each nation to solve all its problems by itself; strict respect for the sovereignty and territorial integrity of all countries; promotion of economic and cultural cooperation on the basis of complete equality and mutual benefit. The CPSU and all other Marxist parties devote a great deal of attention to these lofty tasks.

Consistently implementing the principle of peaceful coexistence, Marxist parties take into account that powerful forces which can safeguard and strengthen peace have arisen and are developing in the world. Alongside the world socialist system which is steadily developing and gaining in strength and is the natural centre of attraction for all peace-loving forces in the world, the extensive zone of peace also includes a large group of peaceable non-socialist countries, many of which had cast off the colonial yoke. A major factor in the struggle for peace is the anti-war movement of the broad masses which are more and more actively taking the solution of the problem of war and peace into their own hands.

The existence of these powerful peace-loving forces has made it possible for the CPSU and the Marxist parties of other countries to reach the conclusion that in our age war can be averted.

The ability of the peace-loving forces to prevent another world war, however, does not mean that every possibility of a war breaking out has been precluded. Such a possibility will exist so long as capitalism exists. Only communist society will establish eternal peace on Earth. In present conditions, however, the unremitting, consistent struggle of the USSR and other socialist countries, and all honest people for peace and security encounters the bitter resistance of reactionary imperialist circles, the military-industrial complex in the first place. Faced with the danger of another world war, the Soviet Union is compelled to take the necessary measures to strengthen its defences and protect the Soviet people and the people of the entire socialist camp.

Peaceful Coexistence as a Form of the Class Struggle

Contemporary opportunists distort the essence of the principle of peaceful coexistence. They consider that peaceful coexistence reconciles the contradictions between the socialist and capitalist systems and spells an end to the struggle between the socialist and bourgeois ideologies.

In reality, however, peaceful coexistence does not at all signify reconciliation of the contradictions between socialism and capitalism and discontinuation of struggle between them. Peaceful coexistence and international detente concern relations between states. "Detente," states the Report of the CPSU Central Committee to the 25th Congress of the CPSU, "does not in the slightest abolish, nor can it abolish or alter, the laws of the class struggle."* Moreover, *peaceful coexistence is a special form of the class struggle between the two opposing world systems*. It is a continuation of the struggle between the two opposing social systems, socialism and capitalism, on the international scene. It is an economic, political and ideological struggle, but in no way a military one. It is waged by peaceful means, without weapons or wars, and without one state interfering in the domestic affairs of another.

Peaceful coexistence is the basis for the economic competition between socialism and capitalism on an international scale. It is a struggle between socialism and capitalism for the trends, rates and scale of economic and cultural growth. In the course of this struggle people find out from their own experience which system can satisfy their needs more fully.

The course and the results of the competition, of the struggle of the two opposing systems determine contemporary world development. It should be stressed that the principle of peaceful coexistence does not signify renunciation of political struggle, of the revolutionary class struggle of the proletariat against the bourgeoisie, renunciation of the working people's struggle for liberation from capitalist exploitation, and of the fight of the

* *Documents and Resolutions. XXVth Congress of the CPSU*, p. 39.

oppressed peoples for national independence, against colonialism and neocolonialism.

Peaceful coexistence of the two opposing systems also implies an irreconcilable ideological struggle, a battle between the socialist and bourgeois ideologies. Socialist ideology which expresses the interests of the working class, of all working people and proves the historical necessity of the proletariat's struggle against the bourgeoisie, for socialism and communism, is the antithesis of bourgeois ideology. It is pitted against bourgeois ideology which expresses the interests of the imperialist reactionary forces, attempts to justify the existence of imperialism and is used as a weapon in the fight against peace, democracy and socialism. All means of ideological influence are exploited for these purposes. The chief of them is *anti-communism*, which mainly consists of slander on socialism and a falsified interpretation of the policies and aims of the communist parties and of Marxism-Leninism. A consistent and implacable struggle against bourgeois ideology is an indispensable condition for the victory of socialism in the peaceful competition with capitalism.

Thus, the existence and development of the socialist system, which opposes more and more successfully the capitalist system, creates increasingly favourable *international conditions* for the growth of the world revolutionary process.

The *internal conditions* too are now more favourable for the transition of more countries to socialism; this is due to the deepening of the general crisis of capitalism and the aggravation of all its intrinsic contradictions.

The Deepening of the General Crisis of Capitalism

While the new world of socialism, full of strength, vigour and health, is growing and advancing, the capitalist system is in the throes of a deep-going process of decline and disintegration.

It is undergoing a general crisis.

This crisis was inaugurated by the Great October Socialist Revolution which resulted in the emergence of the USSR, the world's first socialist state. The undivided rule of capitalism in the world came to an end.

The victory of socialist revolutions in a number of European and Asian countries as a result of which socialism turned into a world system, was another powerful blow sustained by imperialism.

The principal characteristic of the present stage in the general crisis of capitalism is that the correlation of forces in the world has radically shifted in favour of the world socialist system. More and more countries are falling

away from capitalism and the forces fighting for socialism and social progress are rapidly growing throughout the world. The positions of imperialism in the peaceful economic competition with socialism are being inexorably weakened. The unprecedented advance of the national liberation
movement has led to the break-down of imperialism's colonial system.

But contemporary capitalism is trying to adapt itself to the new situation
in the world. In the conditions of the confrontation with socialism, the ruling circles of the capitalist countries are afraid more than ever before of the
class struggle developing into a massive revolutionary movement. Hence,
the bourgeoisie is striving to use more camouflaged forms of exploitation
of the working people, and is ready now and again to carry out partial
reforms in order to keep the masses under its ideological and political control as far as possible. The monopolies have been making extensive use of
scientific and technical achievements to fortify their positions, to enhance
the efficiency and accelerate the pace of production, and to intensify the
exploitation and oppression of the working people.

However, adaptation to the new conditions does not mean that capitalism
has been stabilised as a system. *The general crisis of capitalism has continued to deepen.* The events of the past few years prove this convincingly.

The crisis of capitalism has become all-embracing. A profound crisis
has gripped capitalist economy and politics, ideology and morals. The
sharp cutback in production and the growing unemployment in most of the
capitalist countries intertwined with the monetary, energy and raw materials crises. Impelled by the continuously growing military expenditures,
inflation has made the crisis processes especially acute. The increased
power of the international monopolies has made the competitive struggle
still more ruthless. Capitalism's instability is becoming increasingly apparent. The reformist myth that present-day capitalism is able to get rid of crises has collapsed.

A distinctive feature of the contemporary stage of the general crisis of
capitalism is the deepening of the crisis of imperialism's foreign policy
which is expressed in the loss by imperialism of its decisive role in international affairs.

The politico-ideological crisis of imperialism has also become more
actue. It afflicts institutions of power and bourgeois political parties and
undermines elementary ethical standards. Corruption is increasingly
manifest, even in the top echelons of the state machinery. The decline of
intellectual culture continues and the crime rate is rising.

Bourgeois ideology, too, is in the throes of an intense crisis. Pessimism
and fear of the future, mysticism and mistrust in science and man's creative
powers and abilities, negation of progress, anti-communist slander and

protection of the system of hired slavery and oppression which is hated by the people—such are the main features of this ideology. For a long time now bourgeois ideology has been unable to conceive ideas that would carry away the broad masses; it is an ideology of a class which is on its way out of the arena of history. Therefore its utter bankruptcy is inevitable.

In our time the conflict between the productive forces and production relations in capitalist society has attained the extremes of intensity. Mankind has entered a period of a great scientific and technical revolution. But capitalist relations of production are too narrow for this revolution. Besides inhibiting the development of the productive forces and the application of the achievements of the human intellect in the interests of social progress, capitalism frequently turns them against man himself by converting them into monstrous weapons of devastating war. This profound conflict of the capitalist mode of production confronts mankind with the task of breaking the narrow limits of capitalist relations, unfettering the mighty production forces which man has created and employing them in the interests of the whole of society. The only way to do all this lies through the socialist revolution.

"Imperialism," notes the Final Document of the Moscow International Meeting of Communist and Workers' Parties, *"can neither regain its lost historical initiative nor reverse world development. The main direction of mankind's development is determined by the world socialist system, the international working class, all revolutionary forces...**

The Struggle for Democracy—an Integral Part of the Struggle for Socialism

The expansion and development of the socialist world will continue through more and more countries falling away from the capitalist system.

In the course of the revolution socialist changes are intertwined with democratic, anti-imperialist changes. Lenin, developing and explaining his theory of the bourgeois-democratic revolution growing over into the socialist revolution, maintained that in the epoch of imperialism there could be no "pure" revolutions unconnected with a democratic, anti-imperialist movement of the most diverse social groups. In these conditions the proletariat, the most consistent champion of the popular anti-imperialist aspirations, must head the democratic movement, unite the different classes taking part in it and lead them to the overthrow of the bourgeoisie and the victory of socialism.

---

* *International Meeting of Communist and Workers' Parties, Moscow, 1969*, p. 13.

It is possible that the revolution in a number of countries may pass through two relatively independent stages: general democratic and socialist. This is how the revolution developed in the Soviet Union and some other socialist countries. In the Soviet Union the February bourgeois-democratic revolution preceded the Great October Socialist Revolution. In a number of other socialist countries the revolution passed through an anti-imperialist, democratic phase before entering the socialist phase. The development of the revolution in some other countries where capitalism still holds sway may also proceed in this way.

Powerful democratic movements developed after the Second World War: the national liberation movement and the struggle for the preservation of national sovereignty, the movement for peace and national security and the struggle for democracy in a number of capitalist countries. Contemporary democratic movements are marked by their exceptionally vast scale and organisation. They are spearheaded against imperialism, against the reactionary home and foreign policies of the monopolies.

Of course, the struggle against the monopolies, for peace and democratic reforms is not socialist in character, it does not aim to abolish private property and the exploitation of man by man. But it undermines the rule of the monopolies and facilitates the attainment of national independence and democracy, and thus creates the necessary conditions for undertaking the tasks of the socialist revolution. "General democratic struggles against the monopolies," says the CPSU programme, "do not delay the socialist revolution but bring it nearer. *The struggle for democracy is a component of the struggle for socialism.*" *

The alliance of the working class with all the other working people, and above all with its main ally, the peasants, is being forged in the struggle against the capitalist monopolies, for democracy and peace. Uniting around the working class and its Marxist party, the working people—the peasants, white collar workers and a large number of intellectuals—are schooled in the struggle against reaction. In the course of it they become increasingly convinced that under capitalism they cannot get rid of monopoly oppression and gradually come to the conclusion that the abolition of capitalism is the only way out for them. This is how rightwing socialist, reformist illusions are dispelled and how the political army of the socialist revolution is built up.

It is clear from all this that today the mainstays of capitalism are destroyed not only in the course of the direct social revolution of the prole-

* *Road to Communism,* p. 484.

tariat. Socialist revolutions, national liberation, anti-imperialist revolutions, national democratic revolutions, broad peasant movements, the people's struggle against fascist and other tyrannical regimes, and the general democratic movement against national oppression—all merge into a single world revolutionary process which undermines and destroys capitalism.

Forms of Transition
of Different Countries to Socialism

The question of the concrete forms of transition to socialism by various countries acquires great importance in our age, the age of all mankind's advance towards socialism. What are these forms? What do they depend upon?

Marxism proceeds from the premise that the forms of transition from capitalism to socialism depend above all on the correlation of the class forces in a country. If the forces of the working class and its allies have a decisive superiority over the forces of the bourgeoisie and if the latter realises the futility of resistance, then it may yield power peacefully. History, however, shows that the bourgeoisie is incapable of soberly appraising the correlation of forces; it does not voluntarily surrender its authority and privileges, and resorts to all possible means, including force of arms, to uphold them. This means that the working class must be always prepared to repulse an armed attack by the bourgeoisie and take up weapons to defend its rights.

This, of course, does not mean that a peaceful transition of political power into the hands of the working class is altogether impossible. Such a possibility has always existed, but it was very limited in the epoch of the undivided rule of the bourgeoisie.

After the February Revolution in 1917 Lenin and the Bolsheviks raised the question of a peaceful development of the revolution. This did not happen then, but not through the fault of the proletariat.

Now the situation is different. The new correlation of forces between capitalism and socialism which arose in the world after the last war greatly extended the possibilities of a peaceful transition to socialism. In the capitalist countries themselves these possibilities are rapidly expanding owing to the growth of the forces of democracy and socialism, and the greater influence of the working class and its Marxist parties among the people. In these conditions the working class of some countries, relying on the broad movement of the people against imperialism, has greater opportunities than ever to take power into its hands without bloodshed.

The *parliamentary road* can be one of the ways for the peaceful development of the socialist revolution. If the working class in a number of capitalist countries enjoys the support of the majority of the people and resolutely fights the opportunists, it will be able to win a stable majority in parliament, turn parliament into an instrument serving the working people and, after breaking down the resistance of the reactionary forces, it will be able to create the necessary conditions for a peaceful socialist revolution. The parliamentary way is in this case by no means a reformist way. It is the road of irreconcilable class struggle, *radical revolutionary changes* leading to the building of a new, socialist society.

The peaceful road to socialism, however, should not be absolutised. It ought to be borne in mind that the bourgeoisie is still in power in a large part of the world, that it has weapons which it uses and will continue to use against the working class, against the working people.

Striking proof of this is the tragedy of Chile where the military-fascist dictatorship drowned the people's revolution in the blood of the working people and progressives. Yet, as the Report of the CPSU Central Committee to the 25th Congress of the CPSU states, "the Chilean tragedy has by no means invalidated the communist thesis about the possibility of different ways of revolution, including the peaceful way, if the necessary conditions for it exist. But it has been a forceful reminder that a revolution must know how to defend itself. It is a lesson in vigilance against present-day fascism and the intrigues of foreign reaction, and a call for greater international solidarity with all those who take the road of freedom and progress."*

The working class should always be ready to use both non-peaceful and peaceful forms of struggle. The mastery of all forms, the skillful implementation of those which correspond more to the concrete situation, and the ability swiftly and unexpectedly to replace one form with another, are all essential for the victory of socialist revolution in all countries.

* *Documents and Resolutions. XXVth Congress of the CPSU*, pp. 35-3o.

CHAPTER VIII

National Liberation Revolutions

Socialism signifies complete abolition of exploitation of man by man and liquidation of all, including national and colonial oppression. The struggle against the domination of world capital, for the new, socialist system presupposes destruction of colonialism, a struggle for the independence, revival and burgeoning of nations formerly oppressed by imperialism. In this chapter we shall deal with *national liberation revolutions,* their character, basic objectives, and their significance. First, let us examine the question of the stages of the national liberation movement today.

1. Struggle Against Colonialism and Neocolonialism

Disintegration of Imperialism's Colonial System

Imperialists of a small group of advanced countries not only exploit their own people, but also enslave millions of peoples in other countries. In their time, with the help of bloody armed violence and also deceit, blackmail, and bribery, they laid their hands on the whole of Africa, Latin America and a considerable part of Asia, creating a system of colonialism which until recently oppressed more than half of humanity.

The colonial system of imperialism constitutes one of the grimmest chapters in human history. The death of countless numbers of people, inhuman exploitation, poverty and hunger, disease and benightedness—such was the lot which the imperialists had assigned to the colonial peoples. Suffice it to say that the colonialists were responsible for the enslavement or death of more than 100 million Africans.

The imperialists and their ideologists always talked a great deal about their humaneness and their civilising mission, and that they allegedly bring civilisation, modern technology, culture, a new and better way of life, etc., to the backward peoples. But the oppressed peoples are not taken in by this verbiage. They know that the colonies are a profitable capital investment sphere for the imperialists, a source of cheap raw materials and labour power, commodity markets and extensive military bridgeheads. Exploitation of the enslaved peoples for the sole purpose of gaining maximum profits—such is the essence of colonialism.

Naturally, the peoples could not reconcile themselves to colonial rule: they waged and are continuing to wage a gallant struggle for freedom and national independence.

The Great October Socialist Revolution opened new prospects for the national liberation movement, and gave it a tremendous revolutionary potential; it awakened the oppressed peoples, inspired them to rise and fight, and drew them into the mainstream of the world revolutionary movement. The Soviet Union, the world's first socialist country, became and continues to be a vital source of political and moral support for the oppressed peoples.

The victory of socialism in the USSR and the resulting liberation of more than 100 nations and nationalities from social and colonial oppression, the rout of German fascism and Japanese militarism and the new balance of forces in the world after the Second World War, the rise of the world system of socialism, the growth of the revolutionary movement of the working class and the mounting influence of the communist parties created particularly favourable conditions for the development of the national liberation struggle of the peoples. Imperialism brings the peoples the yoke of colonialism, whereas the emergence of socialism opened up the era of liberation for all oppressed peoples. The succession of socialist and national liberation revolutions has destroyed the old colonial system of imperialism.

However, only the system of open, direct political domination by imperialist states over the bulk of the world population has been undermined.

The Danger of Neocolonialism

Though most colonies and dependencies have won political independence, the liberated peoples cannot feel safe. The imperialists are trying to revive the colonial order and not only to preserve but to intensify the exploitation of the young sovereign states. Tens of millions of people (in the South of Africa) are harnessed to the yoke of colonial oppression. Imperialism continues to be the chief enemy of the national liberation movement; that is why the freedom-loving peoples of the world are determined to fight against imperialism, for real freedom and independence. The struggle against the new forms of colonial oppression, against neocolonialism, is one of the most important tasks of the peoples of Asia, Africa and Latin America.

Neocolonialism is a system of economic, political and also military and ideological measures which the imperialists use to preserve their domination, exercise political control over the developing countries and exploit their economy. Neocolonialism is economic, military, political and ideological expansion of the imperialists in countries whose people have already freed themselves from colonial domination or are fighting for liberation.

For example, the imperialist powers which have retained control over the economy of one country or another strive to intensify its economic exploitation. In spite of the fact that the majority of Asian, African and Latin American countries have won political independence, many of them are still economically dependent on the imperialist powers. A considerable part of the industrial and other enterprises in these countries and the bulk of their natural resources are in the hands of foreign monopolies with the result that they continue to net immense profits from the exploitation of the economically dependent countries. At present the imperialists pump out of them approximately $6,000 million annually in profits alone. One can easily imagine the changes that would have taken place in the national economy and the wellbeing of the population of these countries if these funds were at their own disposal.

Neocolonialism also finds its expression in the economic "assistance" of the imperialists to the developing countries. This "assistance" is by no means unselfish as the neocolonialist ideologists and politicians assert. It has a definite purpose—to impose on the recipient countries economic agreements that would enable foreign monopolies to preserve and strengthen their economic positions and thus subject the economic and political development of these countries to their selfish interests. As a rule, this "assistance" is provided on conditions which impair the national dignity of the recipients; it gives them no chance to choose their own path of development and is a means of pressuring their domestic and foreign policy. Posing as champions of the economic florescence of the liberated countries, the imperialists force them to take to the capitalist road of development and thus keep them in imperialist bondage.

In the struggle against the liberated peoples the imperialists even resort to the export of counter-revolution and direct armed intervention into the domestic affairs of the newly free states.

An important place in the arsenal of measures employed by neocolonialists is occupied by ideological aggression against the forces of progress, socialism and peace. The efforts of the imperialists to continue and intensify the exploitation of the developing countries are supported by the reactionary bourgeois ideology and above all nationalism, a tested weapon of reaction.

As Lenin wrote: "The bourgeois nationalism of *any* oppressed nation has a general democratic content that is directed *against* oppression, and it is this content that we *unconditionally* support."* Such, for example, is the nationalism of some Asian and African countries today; its progressive tendency is manifested in the struggle against imperialism and colonialism, feudal reaction and backwardness, which awakens the awareness of the people, and in the first place, of millions of peasants.

At the same time nationalism is permanently in danger of shedding its democratic content and turning into a reactionary bourgeois nationalism, into Great Power chauvinism and racialism. That explains why the Communists, while supporting nationalism's liberatory trends, are also consistent champions of proletarian internationalism which affirms international solidarity and the friendship of working people of all races and nationalities. Disclosing the decisive role of the class struggle in any social movement, including the national, and urging unity of the working people of all countries, Marxists-Leninists combat the ideology of bourgeois nationalism and cultivate proletarian internationalism in the consciousness of the people.

2. The Character and the Motive forces of National Liberation Revolutions

A national liberation revolution is the highest stage of the national liberation struggle.

The central issue of any revolution, including the national liberation revolution, is that of state power. The struggle of patriotic, national forces of the formerly oppressed nations against foreign monopolies or their stooges is the hallmark of the national liberation revolution.

Like any other revolution, a national liberation revolution breaks out and develops on a definite social and economic foundation. It solves specific tasks and has its own motive forces, i.e., classes and social sections which are active in it.

The Character of the National Liberation Revolution

The economy and political affairs of the colonies and dependencies were dominated by foreign capital which put down any manifestation of political and economic independence, slowed down the development of the

* V.I. Lenin, "The Right of Nations to Self-Determination", *Collected Works*, Vol. 20, p. 412.

economy and deformed it, and turned these countries into its agrarian and raw materials appendage.

The colonies and dependencies were turned into the nearest strategic reserve of imperialism. Quite often they were used as a bastion against the growing forces of world socialism, and a military bridgehead for imperialist aggression. They were an inexhaustible source of cheap raw materials and free labour power, and an extensive and extremely profitable consumer market.

Imperialism not only directly oppresses the people of the colonies and dependencies, and suppresses all their manifestations of political and economic independence; it is also the principal bulwark of internal reactionary forces and above all of the rich landowners and tribal chiefs, the main bearers of feudal and pre-feudal relations.

That is why imperialism and foreign monopolies are the greatest enemies of the oppressed peoples; that is why the national liberation revolutions have a clear-cut *anti-imperialist* character.

The principal aim of these revolutions is to abolish the political and economic domination of foreign imperialism, win political and economic independence and, consequently, set up a sovereign national state.

Yet it is impossible to shake off the oppression of the monopolies without first wiping out the survivals of feudalism and tribal, pre-feudal relations whose bearers were imperialism's principal social mainstay in the colonies and dependencies. That is why national liberation revolutions also have an *anti-feudal character.* Liquidation of the survivals of pre-bourgeois relations inhibiting economic and political progress is yet another important task of the national liberation revolutions.

The solution of such vast and complicated problems is inconceivable without the participation of the people who are the real makers of history. That is why the *uprooting of the survivals of colonial domination in domestic policy and democratisation of social life constitute the third important task of the national liberation revolution* which thus acquires a *democratic character.*

It follows that the national liberation revolution has an anti-imperialist, anti-feudal and democratic character. As Lenin wrote, it solves *"democratic* tasks, the tasks of *overthrowing foreign oppression".* *

The national liberation revolution owes its general democratic, anti-imperialist and anti-feudal character not only to tasks which it sets itself,

* V.I. Lenin, "A Caricature of Marxism and Imperialist Economism", *Collected Works,* Vol. 23, p. 59.

but also to those social forces which are called upon to solve these tasks, i.e., to the motive forces of the revolution. Let us see what these forces are.

The Motive Forces of the National
Liberation Revolution

Before we examine the motive forces of the national liberation revolution we should recall that colonial and dependent countries had different levels of economic and political development. Some of them were agrarian-industrial, others were backward agrarian countries without any industry worth mentioning, while the majority were extremely backward agrarian countries where the survivals of feudal and at times even pre-feudal (patriarchal) relations were still strong.

The social composition of the population of the developing countries is most diverse. All of them have a working class, peasantry, national bourgeoisie and urban petty bourgeoisie, national intelligentsia (civilian and military, and students), feudal lords and a pro-imperialist (compradore) bourgeoisie. With the exception of the pro-imperialist bourgeoisie and the feudal elite all these classes and social forces are oppressed by foreign monopolies and therefore participate in one form or another in the national liberation revolution. Needless to say each class and social group has its own understanding of the tasks of the revolution, and in addition to the national objectives pursues its own social aims.

One of the main motive forces of the revolution is the steadily growing *working class*. It should be borne in mind, however, that its size, unity and level of consciousness vary from country to country. Hence its role and significance in the national liberation revolutions also differ. There are countries where the proletariat has not only developed into a class and achieved organisational and ideological unity, but, guided by Marxist parties, plays the leading role in national liberation revolutions and has ensured their development into socialist revolutions (socialist countries in Asia). In other countries the proletariat is an important motive force of the revolution rallying all the progressive sections of the nation, the peasantry in the first place. There are countries where the proletariat has emerged as a class but so far does not play the leading role in society and has not rallied the nation's progressive forces round itself. Finally, there is another group of countries, mainly African, where the proletariat is only solidifying and organising into a class. Being small in size and weak both organisationally and ideologically, it is as yet unable to decisively influence the course and results of the national liberation struggle.

But in all countries without exception the proletariat, owing to its objective position in society, is the most revolutionary social force which more than any other is concerned with bringing the national liberation revolution to a victorious conclusion. The reason is clear: deliverance from oppression by foreign monopolies and the democratisation of all social and state activity create favourable conditions for the proletariat to attain its historic objective—socialism.

In the course of the national liberation struggle the working class swells its ranks, becomes organised and acquires political experience. Its class awareness enhances and its alliance with the non-proletarian sections develops and strengthens. It forms and consolidates its trade union, youth and other organisations. The national liberation revolutions are a splendid school which prepares the proletariat for its coming social battles for socialism.

The peasantry is numerically the biggest and in some countries the main motive force of national liberation revolutions.

In the colonies and dependencies the peasants were in a terrible, truly desperate plight. Since they had no land they had to lease it from the fabulously wealthy feudal lords and to pay them from 40 to 80 per cent of the harvest.

Moreover, the peasants were harnessed to the yoke of foreign monopolists who owned great tracts of land and, together with the local feudal lords, plundered and ruined the peasants, amassing enormous profits from their exploitation. Peasants who fell into poverty and ruin were deprived of their tiny plots and steadily swelled the already huge army of rural paupers.

The agrarian question is the most crucial social problem in the colonies and dependencies. Their peasants are vitally concerned with abolishing the ownership of the monopolies, local feudal lords and the tribal nobility in land, and with being able to till that land and benefit from the results of their own labour. Naturally, the peasantry is an anti-imperialist and anti-feudal force which is interested in eliminating the political and economic domination of foreign capital and the rule of the feudal-landowner class and the tribal nobility, and in the introduction of radical agrarian reforms.

The status of the *bourgeoisie* in these countries is very contradictory.

It is common knowledge that foreign monopolies and the local feudal lords inhibited the development of the national economy in them. That is why the part of the bourgeoisie which is interested in promoting economic development and is active in the national liberation revolution, particularly in the struggle for political independence, has been named the *national* bourgeoisie, as distinct from the pro-imperialist, anti-national or compradore bourgeoisie which has close ties with foreign monopolies and betrays national interests.

By participating in the national liberation revolution for the sake of its class interests and above all to develop the national capitalist economy and to secure its political domination of society, the national bourgeoisie at the same time expresses certain general national interests inasmuch as it can attain its own class objectives only after liberation from the rule of foreign imperialism and local feudalism. The anti-imperialist, anti-feudal aspirations of the national bourgeoisie result in the coincidence of some of its interests with those of the whole nation and the bulk of the people.

Here it is necessary to take into account the contradictory, dual nature of the national bourgeoisie. Insofar as it is interested in fighting foreign imperialism and internal pro-imperialist forces, the feudal and tribal nobility in the first place, the national bourgeoisie goes along with the people, the working masses, relies on them and uses their revolutionary energy to achieve its own aims. At the same time, however, it fears the revolutionary working class and the peasantry, regarding them as a threat to its exploitatory ambitions and, consequently, endeavours to confine the revolution to its own narrow interests, hold up its development and guide it along the capitalist road.

Self-employed craftsmen, artisans, petty, chiefly retail, tradesmen, and other so-called *intermediate (petty-bourgeois) strata* are very numerous and influential in the developing countries.

In view of the lag in economic development these strata occupy a fairly prominent place in the economy by producing a considerable quantity of consumer goods at their small enterprises, and controlling most of the service industry, retail trade and so forth; and their role in political affairs is equally great. Hence, to a certain extent the future of the national liberation revolution depends on the stand adopted by the intermediate strata, i. e., whether they side with progressive or reactionary forces.

An important, and sometimes the leading role in the national liberation revolution is played by the *national democratic intelligentsia*—men of arts and science, a part of the officialdom, progressive army officers, students, office workers and others. It plays a particularly great role in countries where the working class has not yet consolidated into an independent force and where the national bourgeoisie is either weak or pursues a pro-imperialist policy, as is the case in a number of African countries. Under these conditions representatives of the intelligentsia not infrequently become leaders of the revolution and the state.

3. Winning of Economic Independence—an
Important Task of the Revolution

The attainment of political independence is not the sole task of national liberation revolutions. It is important to consolidate the gains achieved, and put an end to dependence on foreign monopolies but in order to do this it is necessary to win *economic independence*. The ideologists of imperialism, Lenin wrote, usually "are talking of national liberation... leaving out *economic* liberation. Yet in reality it is the latter that is the chief thing."*

Setting Up the National Economy

The imperialists did their utmost to perpetuate their rule in the colonies and dependencies and chain them to their own economic and political system. They nipped in the bud any attempt of the oppressed peoples to develop their national economy, industry in particular.

Imperialism retarded the development of Asian, African and Latin American countries for many decades. With very few exceptions their economies are still at a very low level of development. These countries which account for more than two thirds of the population of the non-socialist world, produce less than 20 per cent of the total output of manufactured goods in the capitalist world, approximately three per cent of machines and equipment and five per cent of metal. Moreover, a considerable part of the industrial enterprises in the developing countries are owned by foreign capitalists.

In order to win economic independence the developing countries have to fight against imperialism's neocolonialist oppression, and to limit and overcome the imposed international division of labour and inequitable economic relations founded on economic plunder of these countries, in the first place by multinationals.

The mounting struggle of the developing countries for new forms of world economic relations, for a *new world economic order,* and for the radical reorganisation of economic relations between them and the imperialist states on a new, equitable and democratic basis, without neocolonialist exploitation, diktat and discrimination, is in fact a struggle for economic emancipation, for the fulfilment of the vital tasks of their economic progress.

---

* V.I. Lenin, "The Social Significance of the Serbo-Bulgarian Victories"*Collected Works,* Vol. 18, p. 308.

The struggle for a new international economic order is supported by the world progressive public, the USSR and other socialist countries in the first place.

Only by delivering their economy from the yoke of foreign monopolies will the peoples of the developing countries be able to assume full control over their vast natural resources and to work for themselves and for the nation, and not for the benefit of foreign imperialists. Only one way leads to the achievement of this goal—*the promotion and development of their own national economy.*

One of the most radical means of shaking off economic dependence and building up a national economy is *nationalisation*, i. e., the conversion of industrial enterprises, transport, communications facilities, banks, commercial institutions and public utilities, schools and other educational establishments into national (state) property. Nationalisation gives rise to the *state sector in the economy.*

India, Iraq, Algeria, Burma, Syria, Mali, Guinea, Ethiopia and other developing countries have nationalised a large number of enterprises, chiefly those which belonged to foreign monopolies and the local pro-imperialist bourgeoisie. Nationalisation and the establishment of the state sector in the economy have made it possible for the liberated states independently to solve certain problems of economic life, influence it and take steps towards the organisation of economic planning. This was a serious blow at colonial exploitation and in many respects deprived foreign capital from exerting a decisive influence on economic development.

When, and this happens quite often, conditions prevent a developing state from promptly nationalising either all or a part of the property of foreign monopolies, the state, in addition to its nationalisation measures, controls the activity of the foreign monopolies for a certain period and curtails their opportunities for exploiting the population and the country's national resources. Frequently mixed enterprises owned by the state and private capital, including foreign capital, are set up.

Economic independence can be attained only through the creation of a highly developed national economy, through *industrialisation.*

Industrialisation ensures the reorganisation of all branches of the economy in the developing countries, including their agriculture, on a modern technical basis, and also makes for high labour productivity. It is a basis on which the country enhances its defensive capability, promotes scientific, technical and cultural progress, and improves the wellbeing of the people.

Many newly free countries are taking the first steps towards industrialisation. With the help of domestic resources and the assistance of other, particularly socialist countries, they are building up their own power base and modern industries, giving priority to those branches which are especially important for the country's efforts to attain economic independence.

The programme for the attainment of economic independence of the newly free countries attaches great importance to resolving the *agrarian question* in favour of the people.

Hence the essence of the agrarian question in the developing countries is to put an end to feudal and pre-feudal relations in agriculture, abolish pre-feudal, feudal and foreign ownership of land, and help the peasants to cultivate this land.

Experience shows that there are different ways of solving the agrarian question. Some newly free countries are carrying out deep-going agrarian reforms aimed at sharply reducing ownership in land and handing over land confiscated from wealthy landowners and foreign imperialists to the peasants. The most radical form of agrarian transformations is the *cooperation of agriculture* which has just started in some of the liberated countries.

The solution of key socio-economic tasks of the national liberation revolution involves a sharp struggle between social forces. The attainment of political independence, which is the content of the first stage of the revolution, was secured by all the patriotic forces of a nation in the struggle against foreign imperialism, while economic independence is won not only in the struggle against imperialism, but also in the contention between various classes and social groups in the given country. In effect it is a struggle for the ways and methods of economic emancipation and the further development of society.

What are these ways? What are the prospects which they open for the newly free peoples?

4. The Path of Socialist Orientation

The choice of ways of development is a matter of great urgency for the liberated people which involves a clash between social forces inasmuch as different classes and parties offer their own solutions. Reactionary circles, above all the wealthy bourgeoisie and the landowners, strive to steer the development of a nation along the capitalist road, and to retain their privileges, private property and continue exploitation by relying on the economic, financial and military assistance of imperialism.

Society's progressive forces, the working class and the labouring peasantry in the first place, strive to protect the people against the intrigues of imperialism and take the country along the road of real independence, welfare and progress.

Taking their own experience into account, the peoples of the newly free countries are becoming more and more convinced that *only the path of non-capitalist development, the path of socialist orientation* leads to national revival and social progress.

The Historical Experience
of Non-Capitalist Development

It was Lenin who substantiated the possibility of the formerly backward countries moving directly into socialism, either bypassing the capitalist stage altogether, or skipping only the stage of industrialised capitalism. He linked this possibility with the rise and development of socialism in other, more advanced countries, whose proletariat is called upon to provide every assistance to people lagging behind in economic and political development. "With the aid of the proletariat of the advanced countries, backward countries can go over to the Soviet system and, through certain stages of development, to communism, without having to pass through the capitalist stage."*

This premise is an application of Marxist theory of the socialist revolution to the specific conditions of countries that have not yet attained the capitalist stage of development and is an expression of all that is specific in the conditions and forms of the transition of these countries to socialism.

Reality has confirmed Lenin's propositions that backward countries could develop along the non-capitalist road. Of the 65 million non-Russians inhabiting Russia in 1917, 25 million lived in the colonial outskirts of Central Asia and were at one or other pre-capitalist stage of development, retaining not only feudal or semi-patriarchal modes of production, but also tribal systems. Thanks to the help of the fraternal nations, the Russians in the first place, these outlying areas in a mere half a century turned into flowering socialist republics with highly developed industry, agriculture and culture. Metallurgical, car manufacturing, electrical engineering and other new, modern industries have been built up there. Agriculture also changed and is now collective and highly mechanised. Cultural backwardness was overcome, and these republics now have their own highly trained national specialists. As regards cultural development, the Soviet Republics

---

* V.I. Lenin, "The Second Congress of the Communist International," *Collected Works*, Vol. 31, p. 244.

not only outpaced the Eastern capitalist countries, but some of the industrialised capitalist countries in the West as well.

The once semi-colonial Mongolia has also traversed the path from feudal backwardness to socialism. It has set itself the aim or turning into an advanced industrial-agrarian state in the nearest future with the assistance of the USSR and other socialist countries.

The experience of the Central Asian Soviet Republics and Mongolia vividly demonstrates what a once backward nation delivered from colonial oppression and exploitation could attain with the help of fraternal peoples. Today it shows the newly-free Asian, African and Latin American peoples how to avoid the terrible phase of capitalist development. It teaches them that the road to real independence and progress is non-capitalist development.

What is, then, non-capitalist development—the path of socialist orientation?

The Substance of Socialist Orientation

Socialist orientation is *the movement towards socialism of countries which have not reached the capitalist stage of development,* a path leading to socialism, bypassing capitalism altogether or the stage of developed capitalism, in conditions of the dictatorship of the proletariat or victory of socialism in other countries.

We know that the transition to socialism takes place as a result of the socialist revolution which requires certain material and class prerequisites (a high enough level of economic development, the existence of mature, politically active working class guided by the Marxist party, etc.). These preconditions usually mature during the capitalist stage of development, and that is why there can be a direct transition to the socialist revolution in advanced capitalist countries.

Things are different in pre-capitalist countries such as are the majority of the young sovereign states. The prerequisites for solving the tasks of a socialist revolution have not yet ripened in them. Therefore, in order to begin moving towards socialism they need a certain period of time to create the necessary material and class conditions. This period in the course of which they launch decisive socialist transformations is an intrinsic feature of socialist orientation.

The socio-economic processes occurring in that initial period (economic development and the corresponding regrouping of the class forces in favour of the labouring masses, the working class in the first place) are in some respects similar to the processes characteristic of capitalist development.

But in a socialist-oriented state they take place at a much faster pace and the masses, which is most important, undergo far less hardships than in the course of capitalist development. At the same time socialist transformations (curtailment of private capital and exploitation, the establishment of people's control over some of the means of production, economic planning, etc.) take place at this initial stage of non-capitalist development alongside changes of a bourgeois-democratic nature, even though their significance is not decisive and they do not determine the socio-economic image of society as a whole. But *whatever their depth or form, socialist transformations are an essential feature of socialist orientation.* If there are no changes of this kind it means that society is developing along the capitalist road.

The unitial stage is followed by a stage of cardinal socialist changes in all fields of social activity, a stage of direct transition to socialism.

Socialist changes become of decisive importance, noncapitalist development becomes fixed and society firmly follows the socialist path. *The national liberation revolution develops into a socialist revolution.*

How soon this new stage sets in depends on the activity of the masses in the revolution, the depth of the democratic transformations in public and state affairs, the growth of the role of the working class and the consolidation of its alliance with the peasantry and on how quickly the leadership of the revolution begins to express the aspirations of the working people.

It is important to note that the path of socialist orientation has become a reality only in the present epoch of mankind's transition from capitalism to socialism and the existence of the world socialist system whose unselfish and all-round assistance bulwarks the countries following the non-capitalist road. "The backward countries can emerge from their present stage of development when the victorious proletariat of the Soviet Republics extends a helping hand to these masses and is in a position to give them support."*

Liberated Peoples Choose Socialism

The experience of broad sections of the People, of the labouring masses in the newly-free countries irresistibly convinces them that the capitalist road is a road of suffering and that socialism alone can bring them freedom and happiness, put an end to the age-old backwardness of their countries, rapidly promote their economy and culture, satisfy their material and cul-

---

* V.I. Lenin, "The Second Congress of the Communist International", *Collected Works*, Vol. 31, p. 244.

tural requirements and forever rid them of exploitation, poverty and hunger and the threat of another world war.

As the revolution gains in depth the bourgeoisie which champions capitalist development proves to be less and less capable of leading the struggle against imperialism and for social progress; moreover, in some countries it has failed to ensure political independence. As regards socio-economic transformations, here, too, it proved to be fatally insolvent. Being an exploiting class it is scared of forfeiting its property and privileges, and is afraid of the revolutionary people. It opposes nationalisation, makes no decisive moves to solve the agrarian question, break up the colonial structure in the economy and public life, and to introduce extensive democratisation. As a result, bourgeois policy is viewed with disappointment and distrust by the people and spurs them to more decisive actions not only against imperialism, but also against the local bourgeoisie.

New life in countries that had liberated themselves from colonial oppression is born in fierce battles against the insidious imperialist opponent, against the forces of internal reaction which with the help of imperialism strive to steer the young states along the capitalist road. But the peoples more and more resolutely link the prospect of full victory of the national liberation revolution, liquidation of age-old backwardness and improvement of life with non-capitalist development.

Expressing the will of the people, their intense desire to build socialism and a new and happy life, the leaders of a number of newly-free countries have made it known that their peoples wish to follow a path of socialist orientation. In Africa and Asia socialist-oriented countries are the vanguard of the national liberation movement.

These countries are carrying out *anti-capitalist, socialist* reforms. By means of nationalisation they build up the state sector and introduce planning principles into economic development. Foreign capital is ousted from the economy; exploitation is restricted; the economic positions of the local bourgeoisie are undermined; the exploiting classes are deprived of the possibility of influencing politics; a national economy is built on the basis of industrialisation; agrarian changes are introduced, particularly agricultural cooperation; an independent, anti-imperialist foreign policy is pursued; friendly relations and cooperation with socialist countries are established, etc.

Much is being done to raise the living standards and culture, promote enlightenment, education, health and the training of technical and scientific personnel.

In the course of the establishment of the national economy, industry in the first place, material prerequisites of socialism—a *modern material and technical base*—are formed. But the creation of material prerequisites also signifies the maturing of social prerequisites of socialism: the development of industry is accompanied by the rise and growth of the working class which comes to play an increasing role in society and forms and strengthens its alliance with the non-proletarian strata, especially the peasantry.

The fact that the working class plays an ever greater role does not mean that always and everywhere, at all stages of the movement along the non-capitalist road it is society's guiding force. Insofar as in a considerable majority of the developing countries the working class is numerically small and organisationally and ideologically weak and is only beginning to enter the arena of political activity, the leadership of the non-capitalist development, especially at its initial stage, may be exercised by revolutionary democratic forces and not by the working class.

The choice of the path of development of the newly-independent countries is accompanied by an acute *ideological struggle*. Among other things this struggle finds its expression in the fact that different classes have their own concept of socialism and the ways and means of building it. At times these views are very far removed from scientific socialism amd are often used to mask the bourgeoisie's efforts to steer the development of one country or another along the capitalist road.

Nevertheless, this does not mean that Marxists, Communists, completely rule out non-Marxist concepts of socialism. These concepts may contain the progressive desire to put an end to capitalism and exploitation and to build a society based on collective ownership. This progressive content, this anti-imperialist and anti-colonial trend of different socialist theories is unconditionally supported by the Communists. At the same time Communists do not merge with diverse social forces working for socialism, and endeavour to bring the theory and practice of truly scientific socialism in to any socialist movement.

It is important that the socialist views of the leaders of some developing countries changed markedly in the course of the national liberation revolution. At first these views were, as a rule, a fantastic mixture of elements of scientific socialism with utopian socialism and religious views, whereas now the leaders of a number of these countries are gradually shifting to positions of scientific socialism.

The evolution to Marxism-Leninism, scientific socialism, is a natural process dictated by the entire course of the national liberation revolution and the objective needs of the developing countries. A truly people's revolution aimed at achieving a country's independence and flourishing, at freedom and the well-being of the people, can win only on the basis of Marxism-Leninism, scientific socialism. "Our revolution has made

Marxism-Leninism its banner," said Fidel Castro, "No one forced us and no one guided us from another continent. Life itself showed us the way and we followed it without hesitation. Every real revolution must inevitably lead to Marxism-Leninism, the only genuine revolutionary truth which repudiates colonial slavery, imperialist domination and exploitation of man by man."

Of course, the progressive part of the revolutionary democracy which is in power does not immediately master Marxism-Leninism. At first it assimilates the individual aspects of Marxism and this is itself a difficult process which is not without deviations and vacillations. But all these vacillations and difficulties can be surmounted only when the revolutionary process whose objective logic has raised a certain part of the revolutionary democracy to power deepens and broadens, and when this objective development of the revolution is correctly reflected in their consciousness.

CHAPTER IX

Social Consciousness and Its Role

in the Development of Society

The material, economic relations of people constitute the basis of social development. But to understand this development, knowledge of the economic factors alone is far from sufficient. Besides productive activity, people and society have an intellectual life. People are guided by definite philosophical, political, moral and aesthetic ideas, they have corresponding scientific theories, and so on. All these ideas and views are of a social character as regards their origin and importance, and belong to the sphere of *social consciousness*.

Social consciousness is of great significance in historical development. To gain a more complete idea of society we have to ascertain what social consciousness is, how it originated and what role it plays in society's life.

1. Social Consciousness—a Reflection of Social Being

The Essence and Origin of Social Consciousness

Social consciousness is the aggregate of people's ideas, theories and views, social feelings, habits and morals reflecting objective reality—the human society and nature. The social being of people is the main object which social consciousness reflects. Since social being is multifarious and complex, social consciousness, too, is multifarious and complex. In the first place we should distinguish social and individual consciousness, social psychology and ideology. In its turn social consciousness has diverse forms—political and legal ideas, morality, art, philosophy and religion. Science, which is also a form of social consciousness, is at the same time turning more and more into a direct productive force of society. Forms of social consciousness arise and develop in their own way, and reflect various aspects of social being. The tasks they fulfil are also different. Idealism is unable to correctly explain the role of ideas, of social consciousness in the life of society. Idealists hold that ideas determine the entire course of social development, but this in no way corresponds to reality.

Only historical materialism, by properly solving the basic question of philosophy as applied to society, has shown that the *social consciousness of people is a product of their social being,* that it is secondary, derived from material, production relations. It is in social being, the material productive activity of people, that we should look for the source of their ideas, theories and views.

The history of society shows that as people's social being, their material production relations, change so does their consciousness; old ideas disappear and new ones arise, conforming to the new conditions, the new social requirements. With the victory of socialism, for example, people's social being changed radically: socialist property replaced capitalist private property. People's ideas and views changed accordingly. For example, instead of the principle of individualism which is the keystone of capitalist morality, the principle of collectivism, the foundation of communist morality, took root.

Similarly, if we analyse any other form of social consciousness we shall find that its ultimate source is the material life of society.

Relative Independence of the Development of Consciousness

Relative independence of the development of social consciousness consists in that it may lag behind the development of social being or run ahead of it; it is also manifested in the continuity of its development; it is not passive in relation to being, but actively influences it.

Social consciousness *lags behind* social being because people's being changes first and only then does their consciousness change. This delay is also conditioned by the great viability of old ideas and views. This viability is not accidental: the ruling classes employ every means at their disposal to thoroughly spread their ideology among all members of society. All mass media (press, cinema, radio, TV, etc.) are utilised, for example, by the contemporary imperialist bourgeoisie to poison the minds of the working people and disarm them ideologically. That is why, after the victory of the new system, survivals of the old ideology persist for a long time in the minds of some people.

The consciousness of people, however, can not only lag behind the development of social being, but under certain conditions can *outstrip* this development. By analysing the laws of society, revealing general tendencies of historical development, outstanding scholars can foresee the future, i.e., create theories which run far ahead of their time and indicate the road of development for many decades ahead. Thus, by studying capitalist reality and the contradictions of its development, Marx reached the conclusion that capitalism was bound to perish and give way to a new, communist society. The Marxist theory of scientific communism is a splendid example of forecasting social events.

Continuity in the development of ideology is an important manifestation of the relative independence of social consciousness. Creating its own ideology, the new class does not renounce past achievements of human thought but assimilates them, places them at its service.

Continuity in the development of ideas is of great importance in social life. If people were unable to use the achievements of the culture of the past, they would literally have to begin everything from scratch: to discover laws which had been discovered long ago, to explore ways of devising the machines they need, ways that had been found long ago, and so on. Thanks to continuity in the development of ideas, this does not happen. Having at their disposal the fruits of the titanic work accomplished by preceding generations, people are able to continue the work of their predecessors, to develop and improve their achievements and raise them to a new, higher level.

Different classes approach the old ideological heritage in a different way. Reactionary classes take from the past reactionary ideas and adapt them to the new historical conditions, to their own interests. The ideologists of imperialism, for example, use medieval scholasticism and mysticism, various idealist and religious systems in order to enslave the working people spiritually.

Advanced, revolutionary classes take from the ideological heritage all that has not lost its positive significance and can promote mankind's progress. The most consistent and devoted custodian of the cultural heritage of the past is the proletariat, whose ideology has assimilated and critically reappraised all the finest achievements of human thought in the course of the long centuries of its development.

The Active Role of Consciousness in
Social Development

Historical materialism, proclaiming the primacy of social being in relation to social consciousness, the ideas and views, social feelings and moods of people, at the same time also admits the *active role* of ideas in the development of society. In any sphere of society's life people always act consciously and purposively and therefore their ideas, views and theories infuse all aspects of social life and greatly influence them. The activity of social consciousness is displayed in that they serve people as a guide to action, unite them and concentrate their efforts on the accomplishment of certain tasks.

People's consciousness, their ideas, can play a dual role by either *promoting* the development of society or *retarding* it. The role ideas play depends on the class that advocates them whether it is progressive or reactionary, or how correctly they reflect the requirements of society's material life and on the extent to which the ideas conform to the interests of the people.

Only ideas which express the interests of the advanced classes of society, of the people, which correspond to the requirements of developing material production and help to abolish the old and establish the new social system, can play a progressive role in society's development.

However new and progressive ideas might be, they are unable, by themselves, to abolish the old social system and create a new one. In order to become a material force, they must grip the minds of the people. Only the people which have assimilated progressive ideas create the social force capable of solving urgent social problems.

Of all the ideas known to the world the most progressive and viable is the Marxist *idea of scientific communism,* of a new social system, without exploitation and slavery, the most just social system on the Earth. It is omnipotent because it is founded on the objective laws governing social development and meets the vital requirements of society's material life and the interests of the millions and millions of working people. That is why the idea of scientific communism has turned into a material force which is transforming the world.

This idea inspired the Russian working class which, in alliance with the poor peasants and under the leadership of the Communist Party, carried out the October Socialist Revolution. It served the Soviet people in their heroic struggle for socialism and is now illuminating their path to the communist morrow. This idea is winning the minds of more and more ordinary people the world over. It is helping the working people in the capitalist countries to fight the reactionary imperialist forces and, where capitalism has been abolished, to build socialism.

As regards backward ideas which distort reality and serve the interests of the reactionary classes, they retard social development. Such, for example, are the ideas of the contemporary bourgeoisie with which it seeks to save the obsolete capitalist system from its inevitable doom.

Dwelling on the active role of consciousness, we should have in mind not only ideas, or ideology, but also social psychology, particularly the psychology of the classes, or large social groups. Social psychology is mass, collective consciousness, so that in many respects the success or failure of one or another historical action depends on the psychological attitude of the people.

Lenin attached very great importance to the psychological factor in history. He studied social feelings and moods of the masses and took them into account in the revolutionary struggle and socialist construction. Following Lenin's behests, the CPSU is concerned with creating a favourable psychological climate in the society as a whole and in all its components which will facilitate the attainment of the tasks facing society.

It follows from all this that people's social consciousness, their ideas, are very important in the life of mankind. In practical activity, therefore, it is important to act not only on the principle of the determining role of social being but also to take into account the active role of ideas in society's development.

2. Individual and Social Consciousness. Social psychology and Ideology

Social and individual Consciousness

Being the consciousness of a concrete person, *individual consciousness* is the mobile totality of his thoughts, views, interests and emotional and other psychic qualities. It is a reflection of the complex interaction of the social environment of the given society and the given individual's concrete, specific environment or micro-environment, a reflection of the universal and individual in the being of people. Moreover, individual consciousness includes *self-consciousness,* i.e., man's awareness of himself, of his relation to the world, society, class and the collective.

The correlation of the social and individual consciousness is a concrete manifestation of the general and the individual in the spiritual life of society. Just as all that is general exists in the individual, social consciousness is manifested only through the individual. This is natural, for only the individual, a concrete personality has the ability to feel and think. In its turn, individual consciousness exists only im connection with social consciousness. Each person lives and works in a society, belongs to a definite class, nation and social collective, therefore his own consciousness is not something that is closed or isolated but also embodies social (class, national) consciousness. This is all the more so because upon entering life he encounters not only ready-made social being, but also social consciousness which he necessarily assimilates to one extent or another and in one form or another.

Social and individual consciousness are one. They have a common wellspring—the being of people; a common basis— practice; and a common means of expression—language. At the same time there are important distinctions in this unity. As compared with individual consciousness social consciousness reflects reality more deeply, more completely. It segregates itself from many concrete, specific features in the consciousness of individuals and absorbs, assimilates only what is common in the consciousness of all individuals. As regards individual consciousness, in addition to the features inherent in the consciousness of one or another social community, it also contains unique features inherent only in a concrete individual and which are engendered by the specifics of concrete being. Since one of the main aims of communist education is to instill communist ideas in the consciousness of each person, it has to take into consideration the specific features of individual consciousness and the individual's mentality.

The elevation of the individual consciousness to the level of social consciousness does not, however, depersonalise the former. Communist equality towards which Soviet society is moving is not equality of depersonalised people with stereotyped thinking, but equality of active and creatively thinking individuals.

Social Psychology

Social psychology is the aggregate of views, habits, feelings, moral features, emotions, illusions and delusions which arise in different classes, nations, social groups and professions under the impact of their *immediate* living and working conditions. For example, the immediate living and working conditions of the working class imbue it with such socio-psychological traits as hostility towards exploitation, awareness of the need to fight against the bourgeoisie, a sense of solidarity, organisation and collectivism. The thirst for profits, individualism and cruelty are the basic features of bourgeois psychology.

Social psychology reflects the position of a class or social collective and their direct objectives and interests. At this stage consciousness is still incapable of broad scientific generalisations and often remains on the surface of phenomena. Marx aptly characterised the state of the consciousness of the working class at the level of social psychology as the state of a "class in itself". It had not yet become aware of its place in society and of its historical mission as the grave-digger of capitalism and the builder of a new, socialist system. It is permeated solely with awareness of its hatred of the bourgeoisie and of the need to fight for its immediate economic interests. Only later, under the influence of socialist ideas and as a result of its participation in the revolutionary struggle, does the working class turn from a "class in itself" into a "class for itself" and becomes capable of scientifically understanding reality and mastering the scientific, Marxist ideology.

Lenin made a profound scientific analysis of the psychology of the bourgeoisie, the proletariat, the bourgeois intelligentsia and the petty bourgeoisie.

Without analysing social psychology it is impossible to understand the history of science and ideology. It is not enough to know the economy of a country in order to understand the history of scientific thought or the history of art in it. One has to be able to turn to *social-psychology* whose careful investigation and understamding are essential for a materialistic interpretation of the history of ideology.

Together with empirical, daily knowledge of the world— nature, society, man—social psychology comprises the first, the lowest level of the reflection of reality called *ordinary consciousness*. This consciousness is amorphous and is not differentiated into definite forms. Political, moral, religious views and knowledge are intertwined in it. In this sense ordinary consciousness is very close to individual consciousness. Nevertheless, it is a *mass, collective consciousness*. It originates spontaneously in large masses of people under the direct influence of the conditions of their life. Ordinary consciousness is the material out of which *scientific, systematised consciousness*, the second, higher level of reflection of reality, is shaped. Ideology and social and natural sciences are scientific consciousness.

A synthesis of ordinary and theoretical consciousness is *public opinion*, i.e., the opinion of people on specific facts of reality—social being, politics and morality, science and religion, literature and art. In these opinions an ordinary, empirical approach to events in social life intertwines with a theoretical, scientific approach. A section of the next chapter treats science, its essence and the role it plays in society. But now we shall examine ideology.

The Class Nature of Ideology

In a class society social consciousness acquires a *class nature*. The totality of political, legal, moral, artistic and other views and ideas of a certain class comprise its *ideology*.

Why does ideology have a class nature? Why does each class create its own distinctive ideology? The reason is that in an antagonistic society the position of classes is by no means identical and that they have differen-

social objectives and tasks. It is by means of a specific system of views that one class or another expresses and substantiates its place in society, protects its interests, strives to achieve its objectives and accomplish its tasks. Bourgeois ideology, for example, protects the interests of the bourgeoisie and endeavours to prove that the principles of private capitalist property and exploitation are eternal. The proletariat, on the other hand, is called upon to destroy capitalism and build socialism and communism—a society without classes and exploitation. In order to do this it needs a qualitatively new, socialist ideology.

This means that a society divided into antagonistic classes cannot have just one ideology. It unavoidably has the ideology of the exploiting class and the ideology of the exploited class, and the dominating ideology is that of the economically and politically dominating class. A bitter ideological struggle which is a form of class struggle is an inherent feature of a class-divided society.

Since ideology always has a class nature, one may ask if it is indeed a true ideology and does not misinterpret reality in order to further class interests. Revisionists maintain that ideology and truth are incompatible, that ideology sacrifices the truth to the interests of one class or another. Marxism, on the other hand, insists that ideology should be approached from concrete historical positions and that it is necessary to ascertain whether it expresses the interests of a progressive or a reactionary class. So long as one class or another plays a progressive role in the sociohistorical process and the interests of this class coincide with the development of objective reality, its ideology is a true reflection of reality. But once a class exhausts its progressive role and its interests clash with the actual course of development, its ideology ceases to be a true ideology and misrepresents reality in order to promote its class interests.

Let us take bourgeois ideology, for example. When the bourgeoisie fought against feudalism, its ideology reflected the world more or less truthfully. But as soon as the bourgeoisie came to power and exhausted its progressive potential, turning into a brake arresting social development, bourgeois ideology lost its ability truthfully to reflect reality. "In place of disinterested inquirers, there were hired prizefighters; in place of genuine scientific research, the bad conscience and the evil intent of apologetic."*

Marxist-Leninist ideology, the ideology of the working class and all labouring people, is the only scientific, true ideology. The class interests of the working class and the objective course of history always coincide, so

* Karl Marx, *Capital*, Vol. I, p. 25

that at all stages of its development Marxist-Leninist ideology preserves its truthfulness.

3. Marxist-Leninist Ideology

Distinctive Features and Significance of
Marxist-Leninist Ideology

Marxist-Leninist ideology radically differs from all the preceding ideologies both in terms of class content, and the aims and tasks which it pursues. The first of these distinctions is that, unlike all the preceding ideologies, it serves the working class and not the exploiting classes, and teaches all working people, the multi-million masses to struggle, work and live for the sake of universal happiness. Secondly, it theoretically substantiates the need to destroy all exploitation and build a classless society—communism. Thirdly, it is profoundly scientific, truthfully reflects objective reality and expresses the vital requirements of society's material life. It is incompatible with a religious or an idealistic world outlook which pervert the true state of affairs. Its theoretical foundation is dialectical and historical materialism. The scientific nature of Marxist-Leninist ideology organically combines with its partisanship and utter dedication to the working class and all working people.

Marxist-Leninist ideology is the most humane in the world. The affirmation of truly humane relations between people and nations, deliverance of mankind from the threat of devastating wars, the establishment of a lasting peace on Earth and a free and happy life for all—such are its lofty ideals.

It advances scientific arguments in support of the need to destroy capitalism and replace the old production relations of domination and subordination with new social relations of concord and mutual assistance. Having arisen in the course of the proletariat's class struggle against the bourgeoisie, it is the former's guide to action in this struggle, it shows the ways and means of building socialism and communism, and is a mighty organising and transforming force.

Marxist-Leninist ideology is able to play its transforming role because it expresses the innermost aspirations and thoughts of the people and, as a result, is widespread among the working class and all working people. Having permeated the consciousness of the many millions of people, it has turned into a mighty material force. Its spread in the masses, however, was not spontaneous but was the result of the gigantic ideological work of the

Communist Party, which combines the ideas of socialism and communism with the revolutionary movement of the masses. The Party upholds the purity of Marxist-Leninist theory in the irreconcilable struggle against bourgeois ideology and revisionism, dogmatism and vulgarisation. It continuously develops this theory on the basis of scientific achievements and socio-historical practice. Thanks to the efforts of the Communist Party Marxist-Leninist ideology has become the *dominant ideology* in the USSR. Embedded as it is in the consciousness of Soviet people it provides them with inestimable assistance in building a developed socialist society.

The Tasks of the CPSU's Ideological Work

It is vitally important for each Soviet citizen to master the fundamentals of Marxism-Leninism, profoundly assimilate the scientific world outlook and fully comprehend the policy of the Party.

The Soviet socialist state draws its strength from the consciousness of the masses. And today methods of persuasion and education and of raising the consciousness of the people to a still higher level are playing an increasing role in the life of Soviet society. The greater the consciousness of the people, the deeper their awareness of the tasks facing them and the higher their activity in the life of socialist society.

Greater consciousness of the people strengthens the ideological and political unity of the workers, collective farmers and the intelligentsia and promotes their gradual fusion into a monolithic collective of the working people.

Ideological education also necessitates the popularisation of the great advantages of socialism over the capitalist system. Today when the problems of the ideological confrontation of the two social systems, the problems of ideological struggle are moving more and more into the forefront, the truth about socialism is a mighty weapon in this struggle.

Increasing significance is being attached to the struggle against bourgeois ideology, reformism and revisionism. The development of economic, scientific, technical and cultural cooperation between countries with different social systems has changed and complicated certain conditions of the struggle against bourgeois ideology. In the first place this is due to the broadening of cultural and scientific exchange. The opponents of communism endeavour to take advantage of this circumstance to intensify hostile propaganda. Naturally, the USSR cannot tolerate such a development. Advocating the promotion of scientific and cultural exchange the USSR at the same time expects that due respect is shown to Soviet laws and customs, and condemns any attempt to interfere in its internal affairs. It maintains that exchange of information should foster mutual understanding between peoples, and widen the exchange of experience and cultural values.

Ideological education is a mighty factor in the struggle for socialism. And only if educational work is closely connected with life, production and the practical experience of the people can it produce positive results and play its part in molding a new person. Nothing adds so much to the stature of the individual as a constructive attitude to life and a conscious approach to one's duty to society, when matching words and deeds becomes a rule of daily behaviour.

In order to educate highly-principled, politically conscious members of society, it is not enough to bring ideas home to the people. What is most important is that the masses should be able to *translate them into reality,* to assimilate them in the form of concrete tasks. It is important that each worker, collective farmer, intellectual, each Soviet person should raise labour productivity, display concern for the preservation of public property, uphold and spread advanced experience and introduce new technology. It is only in work for the benefit of society that one can become a true communist; therefore the fostering of a *communist attitude to labour* and the desire of each Soviet citizen to make a personal contribution to the great cause of communism is a key objective of ideological work.

Concrete deeds are the criterion of the political education. Communist integrity is an alloy of knowledge, convictions and practical deeds. Today's scope of socialist emulation is the result of the fusion of ideological, political and labour education.

The purpose of the party's ideological work is to create such a moral atmosphere in Soviet society that would contribute to the affirmation of respect and care for man, honesty, exactingness towards oneself and other people, and trust combined with strict responsibility and the spirit of comradeship in all walks of social life. The Party wants all Soviet people to live better and work without a hitch.

Today the CPSU and the Soviet Government attach special importance to the communist education of the younger generation. One of the key tasks is to bring it up in the spirit of the revolutionary, labour and combat traditions of the Soviet people. The way to make education more profound was to adopt a *complex approach* to the whole matter of education, i.e., to ensure a well-integrated ideological, political, labour and moral education that would take the specific features of various groups of people into account.

CHAPTER X

Forms of Social Consciousness.

Science

We have ascertained the essence and importance of social consciousness as a whole. We shall now examine its forms and begin with political and legal ideas whose role in social life is particularly significant.

1. Political and Legal Ideas

Politics and economics

Politics, political relations are above all relations between classes, the struggle of classes for power, for domination in society. Relations between states and nations also come within the sphere of politics. Politics arose together with the emergence of classes, the class struggle and the state. Politics is expressed and makes up the *main trend* in the activities of a state.

Politics as the relationship between classes is brought into being by the economic structure of society, its basis. Disclosing the origin of politics and its inseverable connection with the economic structure of society, Lenin called politics the concentrated expression of economics, its epitome and consummation. It is in politics that the economic interests of classes find their fullest and all-round expression.

But politics, while being engendered by economics, itself makes a great impact on the economy, on the entire course of social development. The development of the economy prepares the ground for transforming the social system. This transformation as such, however, is a result of the conscious activity of the people, which is directed by politics. Taking into account the very great role of politics in the life and development of society, Lenin held that politics cannot but have primacy over economics. Of course, this does not refute the indisputable fact that politics is always born of economy and that the economy plays a decisive role in social development. Hence, the solution of economic, production tasks should be approached from the political, class viewpoint. "Without a correct political approach to the matter," Lenin wrote, "the given class will be unable to stay on top, *and, consequently,* will be incapable of solving *its production problem* either."*

It is the political, class approach that distinguishes the activity of the Communist party of the Soviet Union and the fraternal Communist and Workers' parties. In solving any economic and organisational problems, the Communist party always proceeds from the interests of the working class, of all working people. The fundamental interests of the working class, of all the Soviet people dictated, for example, such cardinal transformations as the reorganisation of the Soviet economy along socialist lines, the industrialisation of the country and collectivisation of agriculture.

Political Ideas and Their Significance

People's *political ideas* and *views* are closely connected with politics. While politics expresses the relations of classes, nations and states, political ideas *reflect* and *substantiate* these relations. Political ideas include the views of a class on the class struggle and the revolution, the social and state system, on relations between states and questions of war and peace. These views are applied in the direct struggle of classes, the activities of states, parties and other political institutions and organisations.

Political ideas find their expression in constitutions of states, programmes and declarations of parties and various political organisations, in special theoretical studies and other documents.

The nature of political ideas in antagonistic class societies depends on the interests of the class they express. An exploiting class tries with the help of political ideas to justify its dominant position, to reinforce its economic basis, and this determines the nature of its ideas. An exploited class in its political ideas proves the need for abolishing the exploiting system and creating a new society, a society without exploitation. The political ideology of the exploited is the ideology of revolutionary struggle, of abolishing the old and creating the new.

Two opposing political ideologies—that of the working class and the bourgeoisie—are now at grips in the world. The political ideology of the working class is the ideology of proletarian internationalism, friendship of the working people of all countries, unity and cooperation of all the progressive forces in the common struggle for peace, democracy, national liberation and socialism. It is expressed most fully and from every angle in

* V.I. Lenin, "Once Again on the Trade Unions, the Current Situation and the Mistakes of Trotsky and Bukharin", *Collected Works*, Vol. 32, p. 84.

the Marxist-Leninist theory, in the Communist parties' programmes and the socialist countries' Constitutions. This ideology proves the need for the class struggle of the working class and all the working people against the bourgeoisie, the necessity of the victory of socialism and communism. It serves the working class and its party as a guide in the political struggle, the highest form of the proletariat's class struggle.

The policy and the political ideas of the working class are truly scientific. They are founded on knowledge of the laws of social development and fully correspond to the interests of the people. The experience of history and the great successes of the world communist and working-class movement demonstrate the strength and vitality of these ideas.

Pitted against the political ideas of the working class are the political ideas of the imperialist bourgeoisie, whose aim is to sanctify and perpetuate capitalist wage slavery and prop up the decayed economic basis of capitalism. These ideas seek to justify the policy of suppression of the working class and the democratic forces within the country, the policy of national oppression and aggression.

The political ideas of the contemporary reactionary bourgeoisie have no scientific basis. They run counter to the objective laws of social development and the interests of the people, and are therefore doomed to failure. Just as the nazi idea of world domination failed, so the ideology and policy of colonialism and neocolonialism is collapsing before us, and so will all the other reactionary ideas of the contemporary imperialist bourgeoisie.

Of all the forms of social consciousness, politics and political ideas stand closest to the economic basis. Through the activities of the state, of parties and other political organisations, politics and political ideas influence the basis and the entire course of social development. Moreover, they especially affect the development of all other forms of social consciousness—law, morality, art, religion, philosophy and science. They permeate all these forms of social consciousness, give them a class bias and turn them into the tool of a certain class.

Politics and political ideas play an especially important role in a socialist society. Thanks to the domination of public ownership and the planned economy under socialism the Soviet state and the Communist Party are able consciously to guide the entire course of social development. The policy of the CPSU is the vital foundation of the socialist system. It formulates domestic and foreign policy, sets the people definite tasks and mobilises the working people for their fulfilment in strict conformity with the objective laws of social development. The ultimate aim of the CPSU policy is communism and it directs the work of the state machinery, Party and public organisations and diverse methods of ideological influence towards the attainment of this goal.

Law and Legal Ideas

Besides political, legal relations, regulated by law, exist in society. *Law* is the totality of *obligatory* standards and rules of behaviour of people in society. These rules are expressed in corresponding laws which are safeguarded by the state and all its numerous instruments of compulsion and education.

Law, like politics, arose with classes and the state. It is the will of the ruling class expressed in legal forms and it defends the political and economic interests of the ruling class.

The history of antagonistic class society has known slave, feudal and capitalist law, each of which served the exploiters in their struggle against the exploited. Only socialist law expresses the interests of the working people and is the true law of the people.

People's legal relations should be differentiated from their legal ideas and views which describe the attitude of people to the law of the given society and also their concepts of what is lawful and unlawful, obligatory or nonobligatory as applied to people, states and nations.

Legal ideas and views bear a class character and express the interests of a definite class. In an antagonistic class society the legal ideas of the exploiting class prevail. In order to impose its will on the other classes the ruling class uses not only the state machine, but also legal ideas. By means of these ideas it tries to justify the law it has established, conceal its class character and present it as the law of the whole people, as the supreme expression of justice and good.

Let us take capitalist society as an example. It has a system of law founded on the legal ideas of the bourgeoisie. The purpose of these ideas is to prove that society can have no fairer law than bourgeois law, that it is an embodiment of democracy, that the bourgeois court is impartial, etc. In reality bourgeois law protects capitalist property and serves to justify exploitation and the suppression of all progressive forces.

With the appearance of the socialist state, socialist law is born, the first law in the history of society which rules out class inequality of people.

Socialist law and the legal ideas underlying it radically differ from the law and legal ideas of antagonistic class societies. They express the interests of the entire people, protect and help to consolidate the economic basis of socialism, socialist property, and teach Soviet people to observe the law and conscientiously do their duty. The socialist system is incompatible with lawlessness and contempt for the interests of the individual, and therefore the Soviet state and the Communist party constantly reinforce socialist law and order and brook no attempts to violate it.

Since the laws of socialist society fully correspond to the working people's interests, the absolute majority of Soviet citizens comply with them consciously and voluntarily, and the Soviet state applies measures of compulsion only against those who maliciously violate public order, embezzle social property or commit other crimes.

As society advances to communism the role of the state as a force compelling the citizens to observe the law will diminish and its functions of preserving socialist law and order will be gradually transferred to public organisations. Their task will be not so much to find and punish the violators as to prevent violations and teach Soviet citizens to respect the law and consciously uphold it.

In the future, as a result of the improvement in the people's material and cultural standards, the rise in their social consciousness and organisation, all the conditions will be created for eliminating violations of the law and fully replacing criminal punishment by public reprimand and corrective education. With the complete victory of communism there will be no need for law. Law will naturally merge with the duties and rules of the communist way of life.

2. Morality

The Essence of Morality and
Its Place in Social Life

Morality or *ethics* is the aggregate of standards or rules of behaviour in society, reflecting people's ideas of justice and injustice, good and evil, honour and dishonour, etc. In contrast to legal standards, moral standards and rules are not recorded in laws, but are maintained by force of public opinion, customs, habits and education, by force of man's conviction. They determine man's attitude to society, to the family and other persons and other nations.

Morality arose with the birth of human society. Society has always made definite demands on its members expressed in moral standards. These standards are not eternal. They change with society's development under the influence of changes in production and above all in relations of production. In primitive society moral standards were equal for all members. With the appearance of classes they began to reflect the interests of one class or another. Morality acquired a class character. In a society divided into antagonistic classes there exist the morality of the exploiters and the morality of the exploited, the morality of the ruling class prevailing: under slavery, the morality of the slaveowners dominated; in feudal society, the morality of the feudal lords, and in bourgeois society, the morality of the capitalists. They are opposed by the moral standards and principles of the slaves, peasants and proletarians.

As an element of the superstructure, morality influences all aspects of life in society. Through the attitude of the people to work and property, it influences the economy. Communist morality, for example, by declaring socialist property sacred and inviolable, stands guard over the economic foundation of socialism. Morality also has a direct bearing on politics; any political action of a state receives moral appraisal, approval or disapproval from the members of society. It is natural that the people's moral approval of a political action is an important factor making for its success. The success of the Soviet Union's peace policy is largely due to the moral support of the peoples of all countries, all progressive mankind.

At present, two moralities are pitted against each other in society: communist and bourgeois. What is their essence? What social problems do they solve? Bourgeois morality, which protects the interests of the imperialist bourgeoisie, plays a reactionary role in society's development. Its main social aim is to preserve the keystone of capitalism, private property and exploitation.

Bourgeois morality is conditioned by the dominance of private capitalist property which disunites people, turns them into enemies, rivals in the struggle for profit, the holy of holies of capitalism. In the quest for profit the capitalist tramples upon all standards of human morality; he is absolutely indifferent to the fate of the people around him, to the fate of his country and society as a whole. He places his selfish interests above everything else in the world. Extreme selfishness is the basic principle of bourgeois morality. "Man to man is a wolf", "Everyone for himself and the devil take the hindmost"—these are the ethical rules proclaimed by the morality of bourgeois society. There could be no other rules in a society where private property holds sway, where money is the supreme moral measure, where everything— love and honour, the dignity and conscience of man—is bought and sold.

The spirit of individualism, self-interest, the thirst for profit, hostility and competition make up the essence of the ethics of capitalist society. The exploitation of man by man, on which bourgeois society rests, is the grossest violation of ethics.

Morality in socialist society

The world's most progressive, humane and noble morality is *communist morality*. It expresses the interests of the absolute majority of members of society, the interests and ideals of all working people, and not merely the interests of a handful of exploiters.

Communist morality embraces ordinary standards of human behaviour which the people formulated in the course of their struggle against exploitation and vice. It is common knowledge that the distinctive features of people of labour have always been straightforwardness, honesty, willpower and courage; they fulfil their obligations to one another, to the family and old people. In the struggle against exploitation and in joint labour they developed such moral qualities as mutual assistance, fraternal solidarity and intolerance of slackers and parasites. These qualities are the foundation of those *simple moral standards* which were handed down over the centuries by one generation to the other. An especially important role in the moral development of society, in the formulating of the standards and requirements of the communist morality is played by the morality of the working class, the most progressive class of our age, the creator of the new, communist society.

Communist morality originated under capitalism where it expressed the protest of the proletariat against exploitation and inequality, its desire to introduce rules of human behaviour based on friendship, comradely cooperation and mutual assistance of people free from capitalist slavery. But in capitalist society the morality of the working class, of the working people, does not hold sway. It begins to prevail with the abolition of capitalism and the establishment of a socialist society. The domination of the principles of communist morality in the USSR is a result of the victory of socialism, of the enormous organisational and educational work of the Communist Party and the Soviet state.

Communist morality, Lenin pointed out, is subordinated to the interests of the proletariat's class struggle, whose *content and aim is to build and consolidate communism*. It is this idea of Lenin's that underlies *the moral code of the builder of communism*, formulated in the Programme of the CPSU. From the point of view of communist morality, that which promotes the movement of society towards communism is moral. *Devotion to the cause of communism, love of the socialist motherland* which blazes for mankind the trail into the communist morrow, *love of all the socialist countries*, is the first, cardinal demand in the moral code of Soviet citizens.

Labour is the source of society's wealth and the personal wellbeing of each member of socialist society; labour is the duty and matter of honour for each Soviet citizen. That is why *conscientious labour for the good of society, concern on the part of everyone for the preservation and growth of public wealth* are prime demands of communist morality. The overwhelming majority of Soviet citizens live up to these demands; for them the rule of socialism—he who, does not work, neither shall he eat—became law long ago. Work for the benefit of their homeland is a source of genuine joy and happiness for the Soviet people.

The lofty principles of communist morality stem from the very nature of the socialist system, from its economic basis, public ownership of the means of production. It unites people, enables them to live and work according to the principles of fraternal friendship, mutual respect and cooperation. Hence such an important principle of communist morality as *collectivism and comradely mutual assistance* expressed in the slogan: one for all and all for one.

The principle of collectivism means that the main thing in man's behaviour is to serve society, the collective, to subordinate his personal interests to public interests. Socialism affirms a morality which is basically unlike the morality of capitalism, a morality of cooperation and collectivism, friendship and mutual assistance. The most important demand of this morality is to promote the wellbeing of the people and the all-round development of the individual in conditions of collectivism. It is important to note that in socialist society concern for the social interests does not run counter to the interests of the individual. Everything good done by a Soviet citizen is done both for himself and for all the people. Being conscientious in his job he thereby shows his concern for his comrades who also work for the good of all. This strikingly reflects the combination of the social and personal interests in socialist society. The aim of socialist production is to satisfy man's requirements. The desire to be useful to society, to one's people primarily motivates the actions of the Soviet citizen.

The principle of collectivism underlies the approach to duty, conscience and honour. It is man's duty and honour to be *intolerant of actions harmful to the public interest,* to be useful to society, to contribute to its advance. If a man does everything in his power for society, for the good of the people, his conscience is clear and he has a *high sense of civic duty.*

The development of proletarian internationalism, of socialist patriotism and humanism is an indispensable condition for implanting the principles of communist morality in the minds of the Soviet people. Socialist humanism is of a higher, qualitatively new type. It consists of genuinely *humane relations and mutual respect.* man is to man a friend, comrade and brother. Socialist humanism combines respect, love for man and concern for his material and spiritual welfare with *vigilance* and an *uncompromising attitude to the enemies of communism, peace and the freedom of the nations.*

Soviet patriotism, too, is qualitatively new. It combines love for, and devotion to, one's country, to the entire socialist community with proletarian internationalism, *fraternal solidarity with the working people of all countries, and with all the nations* and respect for the people of all other states, big or small. Soviet patriotism is incompatible with nationalism, the ideology of national isolation and hostility between the peoples, national inequality and disunity of the working people. The morality of socialist society proclaims the *friendship and brotherhood among all the peoples of the Soviet Union and condemns national and racial hatred.*

Communist morality demands that people observe the rules of the socialist way of life, calls for a courteous attitude towards older people and women, *mutual respect in the family and concern for the upbringing of children.* Love, equality and mutual assistance between husband and wife, friendship and mutual trust of parents and children comprise the ethical foundation of the family in socialist society.

The principles of communist morality also require definite traits in man's character: *honesty and truthfulness, moral purity, simplicity and modesty in social and private life, an uncompromising attitude to injustice, parasitism, dishonesty, money-grubbing and careerism.*

Elimination of the Survivals of Capitalism— an Integral Part of Communist Education

The success of socialist construction and the Party's tremendous educational work have made the principles of communist morality part and parcel of the Soviet people's life and work. But survivals of the past still persist in the minds of some people. There are still human drones who have no desire to work and prefer to lead a parasitic life, money-grubbers, selfish individuals and bureaucrats who place their private interests above everything else. There are also embezzlers of socialist property and violators of labour discipline and public order.

Why do survivals of the past persist in the consciousness and behaviour of members of socialist society?

In the first place, socialism does not grow up on its own basis, but emerges from capitalism which carries its traditions and customs over into the new society. Social consciousness does not change at once following changes in social being, but only after a certain time, as a result of which it may lag behind social being. It is, therefore, clear why the old traditions and habits weigh upon the people of the new society for quite along time.

Furthermore, the existence of backward views is in no small way due to the influence of the ideology of the bourgeoisie which does everything possible to affect the minds of Soviet people, to revive bourgeois customs and prejudices.

Yet it would be a serious error to think that capitalist influence alone is responsible for anti-social behaviour and views under socialism. Certain causes for their existence are to be found in the socialist society itself, including the presence of some elements of economic and social inequality, absence of equal conditions for the life and development of all members of society, violations of socialist laws; in particular, the law of distribution according to work done, weakening of control over the measure of work and consumption, and shortcomings in ideological work and in the education of the rising generation in the family and at school. So far not all violations of Soviet laws and principles of Communist morality are censured by the broad public.

Survivals of the past are extremely tenacious. They do not wither away of themselves and persist for a long time in the life and consciousness of millions of people even after the economic conditions which engendered them have vanished. Taking all this into consideration the Communist party views the struggle against the survivals of the past, against manifestations of bourgeois ideology and morality, and against the survivals of proprietary mentality as a *component of communist education*. The higher the level of Soviet society in its development, the more intolerable are the still occurring departures from the socialist rules of morality. Acquisitiveness, proprietary tendencies, hooliganism, red tape and indifference to one's fellow humans run against the very grain of the socialist system. In combating such phenomena, there is a need to make full use of the opinion of the work collective, criticism in the press, methods of persuasion and the force of the law.

And here an important role is played by the Soviet public, by Party, Komsomol, trade-union organisations, in fact by every Soviet citizen. Public opinion, criticism and self-criticism, friendly censure of anti-social behaviour are gradually turning into the main means of uprooting bourgeois views, morals and customs. The power of example in public affairs, in private life, and in the performance of one's duty acquires tremendous educational importance.

All work for the good of society, both manual and mental, is respected in the Soviet Union. Social labour is the duty of each Soviet citizen. Man's consciousness is gradually transformed and his lofty spiritual traits—collectivism, industriousness, concern for the preservation and growth of public wealth, humanism and comradely mutual assistamce—are moulded in the course of the planned collective labour and the daily participation of all members of society in running state and public affairs. Man's abilities and talents develop in the process of work, he advances culturally and technically, becomes imbued with the spirit of pioneering, creativity and love for the new, and learns to place the interests of society above everything else. That is why the fostering of a communist attitude to work, based on the finest examples of labour and economic management, is one of the most important means of bringing up people in the spirit of the lofty principles of communist morality.

Persistent study, constant advance in general education and culture help eliminate survivals of the past in people's minds. The more cultured and educated a person is the more efficiently he works and the more actively he participates in public affairs.

3. Religion

The Essence of Religion and Its Role in Society

Religion is a distorted reflection of reality. "All religion ... is nothing but the fantastic reflection in men's minds of those external forces which control their daily life, a reflection in which the terrestrial forces assume the form of supernatural forces,"* Engels wrote.

The opponents of Marxism attempt to prove that religion is eternal, that nature endowed man with religious feelings. In reality, however, religion arose only at a definite stage in society's development. The origin of religion can be traced to ignorance of the true causes of natural and social phenomena, to the awe-inspiring power of nature's spontaneous forces and to social oppression.

The basic feature of religion is belief in the supernatural. Being dependent on nature's forces, men ascribed supernatural properties to them, made them into gods and spirits, devils and angels, etc. They naïvely believed that if these imaginary beings were not appeased, they could inflict harm and suffering on them, while if they were placated and worshipped they would help the people. This is how religious worship arose, a combination of prayers, sacrifices and other rites. Religious worship brought into being priests, sorcerers, pastors and other religious servants and also various religious organisations and institutions.

---

* Frederick Engels, *Anti-Dühring*, p. 382.

The appearance of classes and exploitation subjected man to the pressure of spontaneous social forces in face of which he was as helpless as the savage was in face of elementary natural forces. The helplessness of the exploited in the struggle against the exploiters, Lenin wrote, gave rise to a belief in a better life in the next world as inevitably as the impotence of early man in fighting nature engendered belief in gods, devils, miracles, etc. The working people sought in religion salvation from the terrible sufferings and privations inflicted on them by exploiting society.

The social role of religion can be either progressive or reactionary because it is used for political ends by different social classes and groups.

The exploiting classes use, and have always used, religion as an instrument of spiritual oppression, subordinating the working people to their interests, and buttressing their own dominant place in society.

"Religion is the opium of the people—this dictum by Marx is the cornerstone of the whole Marxist outlook on religion,"* Lenin wrote. It preaches subordination to the exploiters, submission to fate, non-resistance to evil and violence, and thereby paralyses the people's revolutionary energy, dooms them to passivity, to patient waiting for everything to be done by god's will. By its false promises of the kingdom of heaven, of a happy life in the next world, religion diverts the working people from the most burning issues of reality, from the revolutionary struggle against exploitation and for a just, genuinely humane social system.

Today religion is a weapon used by reactionary imperialist forces. At the same time, however, clerics are compelled to reckon with the new historical conditions, with the desire of the people for peace—and their craving for a better life. And so, in order not to repulse the believers and to swell their numbers, clerics in some measure take the interests of the people into consideration, especially their striving for peace and material security. But this does not as a rule alter the social functions of religion which under capitalism continues to be an instrument of the exploiters in their struggle against the working class, against the forces of socialism and progress.

It occurs in history that one and the same religion plays different roles in society, depending on what class practises it. For the mass of the people, for example, Islam is an ideological weapon against reactionaries, while reactionaries and imperialist forces often use it against the progressive forces.

---

* V.I. Lenin, "The Attitude of the Workers' Party to Religion", *Collected Works*, Vol. 15, p. 402-03.

It is, therefore, wrong to refer a movement to the reactionary camp just because its slogans are religious. In our time, priests and large masses of believers often come out for social progress, and against reaction. There are a variety of reasons (low level of political awareness, strong religious traditions in the country, religious education, and the like) why progressive action is clothed in religious garb, as is indeed typical for developing countries.

Marxism-Leninism argues that joint struggle against reaction and for a revolutionary renewal of the world by all the working people—believers and atheists alike—is necessary and possible. Communist parties in developing countries organise cooperation with the mass of believers in the fight against imperialism, and for peace, democracy and socialism. For Communists, wrote Lenin, "creation of a paradise on earth is more important... than unity of proletarian opinion on the paradise in heaven".

Religion is deeply hostile to science, to a scientific world outlook. For many centuries the Church ruthlessly suppressed science and persecuted scientists. It prohibited the spreading of progressive ideas, destroyed books propagating these ideas, and confined their authors to dungeons or burned them at the stake. Many progressive people perished in the flames of the Inquisition, including such notable scientists as Giordano Bruno and Lucilio Vanini.

Despite all its exertions the Church was unable to stem scientific progress dictated by the requirements of material production. In our days, being unable to refute the greatest scientific achievements, the clerics try to reconcile science with religion, to prove that scientific achievements do not run counter to faith, but are in line with it.

Such attempts are absolutely futile. Science and religion are incompatible. Science gives man true knowledge of the world and the laws of its development. It helps him to master natural and social forces and to organise production. Religion, on the other hand, distorts the essence of the world, gives the wrong interpretation of it, stultifies the mind and will of man and deprives him of confidence in the triumph of science and progress.

4. Art

*The Main Features of Art and Its Role in
the Life of Society*

Art is a form of reflection of reality in artistic images in the mind of man. Reflecting the surrounding world, art helps people to understand it and serves as a powerful instrument of political, moral and artistic education.

The diversity of phenomena and events and also the different methods of reflecting them in works of art have given rise to diverse kinds of art: poetry and fiction, theatre, music, the cinema, architecture, painting, sculpture.

The cardinal feature of art is that, in contrast to science, it reflects reality not in concepts, but in a *concrete form perceivable by the senses,* in the form of typical artistic images. The artist creates an artistic image, reveals common, essential features of reality and conveys these features through individual, often inimitable characters, through concrete phenomena of nature and social life. The more vivid, the more tangible the individual traits of the artistic character, the greater its attraction and influence.

Art appeared at the dawn of human society; it arose in the process of labour, in the course of man's practical activity. Initially art was directly intertwined with labour. To this day it has preserved this connection, though in a more mediated way. Truthful art has always been a real aid to people in their life and work. It has helped them fight the forces of nature, brought them joy and inspired them to feats of labour and exploits in battle.

Aesthetic tastes and requirements, appreciation of beauty in life and in art developed in the process of labour. One of the primary distinctions and tasks of art is to seek out the beautiful in life, to generalise it, typify it, mirror it in artistic images and bring it to man, satisfying his aesthetic requirements and developing his aesthetic emotions.

In a class society art bears a class character, it is partisan. There is no "pure" art, no "art for art's sake", nor can there be any. The accessibility, the great power of conviction and emotional impact of art make it an important weapon of the class struggle. That is why classes exploit art as a vehicle of their political, moral and other ideas.

Art is part of the superstructure and it serves the basis on which it develops. Contemporary bourgeois art, for example, serves the reactionary imperialist forces. It seeks to divert the working people from struggle against the exploiters, fosters in people immoral traits, contempt for other peoples and countries and for the forces of peace and progress. Bourgeois art is employed to glorify the capitalist order of things and slander communism and the communist movement. Defending the interests of obsolescent classes, this art departs from the truth of life and becomes formalistic and devoid of content. Among contemporary artists in capitalist countries there are also realists who reflect life truthfully and profoundly, but they are often hounded by the ruling imperialist circles.

Each class creates an art that corresponds to its class interests and aesthetic requirements. But among works of art there are many which have survived their class and age. These are works which vividly and truthfully reflect lasting, general traits inherent in people of the most diverse eras, and also works which make it possible to understand the essence of an era or a class. Among them are the finest sculptures of ancient Greek masters, paintings of the Renaissance, the works of 19th century Russian composers and many other works of art which long ago became the possession of all mankind. From this follows another distinction of art, continuity of its development. The art of each new era preserves all that was progressive and good in the art of the preceding eras.

Socialist Art

A qualitatively new, socialist art has arisen on the basis of the revolutionary struggle of the working class and its advance to communism. Socialist art assimilates the best from progressive art of the past and constitutes a higher stage in the development of art corresponding to the new historical conditions.

Socialist realism is a creative method of this art. The main content of our age must be reflected truthfully, in a historically concrete and highly artistic way. The art of socialist realism does not stand still but is constantly developed and enriched.

The basic principles of the art of socialist realism are *truthfulness* and *profundity* in the reflection of reality, close *bonds with the people, partisanship* and *bold pioneering* in the artistic portrayal of life, combined with the use and development of all the *progressive traditions* of world culture. Socialist realism is conspicuous for its profound socialist content and diversity of vivid national forms. The method of socialist realism affords writers, painters and other artists vast scope to display their creative initiative and high mastery, and to develop numerous creative forms, styles and genres.

Truly realistic art has always been linked with the people, rooted in them, but the organic ties of socialist art with the people, with their life and work are unprecedented. Pointing out the popular character of socialist art, Lenin once said: "Art belongs to the people. Its roots should be deeply implanted in the very thick of the labouring masses. It should be understood and loved by these masses. It must unite and elevate their feelings, thoughts and will. It must stir to activity and develop the art instincts within them."*

The popular character of socialist art is organically combined with its partisanship. Soviet art openly and directly serves the working class and all the working people. It has linked its destiny with the Communist Party, with the Marxist-Leninist world outlook.

Revisionists attack the Marxist-Leninist principle of partisanship in art; they oppose the guidance of art by the Communist Party, claiming that this suppresses the creative freedom of the artist, his artistic individuality, and so on and so forth. In reality, however, the principle of partisanship ensures the lofty ideas, content and high artistry of socialist art, and orients it at the solution of the most pressing social problems. It is an indispensable requisite for genuine freedom of artistic endeavour.

The Communist Party expends great effort on developing socialist art. It constantly promotes among the artists the spirit of devotion to the people, to the cause of communism and an irreconcilable attitude to shortcomings, lack of political awareness and of ideas and content in art. The CPSU has set itself the task of steadfastly promoting the burgeoning of literature and art, the aesthetic education of the people and the cultivation of high artistic tastes and traits.

The mission of Soviet art is to foster in people lofty political, moral and aesthetic traits; to help eradicate survivals of the past from their minds; to deeply and truthfully portray the heroic labour and struggle of the people; to reveal the rich spiritual world of our contemporary, his thoughts, feelings and aspirations; to flay implacably everything that hinders the onward movement of Soviet society; to inspire the Soviet people to fresh exploits in the construction of communism. Art plays a particularly great role in the *aesthetic* education of the people and is an important component of communist education. Art must develop appreciation of beauty, aesthetic emotions in all Soviet people, and awaken and develop their artistic abilities and tastes.

The development and enrichment of the art are based on a combination of mass amateur art endeavour and professional art.

5. Science

Science as a Form of Social Consciousness

* V.I. Lenin, *On Literature and Art*, Moscow, 1975, p. 230.

As a form of social consciousness, science *is a system of man's knowledge of nature, society and thought.* It reflects the world in concepts, categories and laws, whose truth is verified by practical experience.

Contemporary science as a whole is a totality of different sciences studying concrete spheres of the material reality. In this diversity of sciences it is necessary to single out *social* sciences, such as history, political economy, philosophy, aesthetics, etc.—and *natural* sciences—mechanics, mathematics, physics, chemistry, biology, etc. A distinctive feature of the development of contemporary science is the growing *differentiation,* i.e., the division or fragmentation of the traditional sciences into ever new branches and trends. Take biology, for example. Once the single science studying living organisms, it has given rise to genetics, ecology, the evolutionary theory, microbiology, physiology and others.

Differentiation of sciences is indissolubly linked with the *integration* of sciences, i.e., the emergence of new disciplines synthesising the achievements of two or more sciences. Such are physical chemistry, chemical biology, biomechanics, cybernetics, bionics and others. Today the most important discoveries are more often made at the junction, the "border" of sciences. Such, for example, was the deciphering of the genetic code and the establishment that the structure and properties of the organism depend on the composition and pattern of the biochemical components of the germ cell. This discovery was made at the junction of biology, chemistry and physics.

Historically, science arose out of practice and is developing on its basis. Of course, science has its own sources, its inner logic of development, but its principal motive force are *social requirements,* the requirements of material production in the first place. In primitive society man, while gaining the means of subsistence, encountered the forces of nature which gave him his very first, superficial knowledge. This knowledge was empirical and was not yet science. As a special form of social consciousness science arose later, in the slave-owning society, when mental labour became separated from manual labour and a special group of people—scholars, who engaged only in study, appeared.

An important feature of science is the *continuity* of scientific knowledge. Each new generation of people, each newly formed society does not discard past scientific achievements, but assimilates and develops them in conformity with the new requirements of practice and with science itself. Thus, scientific knowledge belongs to humanity as a whole and scientific research is social labour.

To a large extent scientific development depends on the economic relations which are dominant in a society and on the nature of its sociopolitical system. They determine the aims, direction and the pace of the development of science and the application of its achievements in society. Capitalist relations of production were a mighty factor of scientific development in the period of the establishment of capitalism when the rapidly growing capitalist production needed more and more scientific knowledge. But with the advent of imperialism these relations became an obstacle to scientific progress.

Social sciences which express the interests of a certain class are in particularly great dependence on society. For instance, bourgeois sociology defends the capitalist system, embellishes its crumbling façade and attacks socialism and social progress. It does its utmost to uphold and disseminate an idealistic and religious world outlook and imposes idealistic and metaphysical methodology on natural scientists. Of course, many scientists in bourgeois society condemn imperialism and adhere to positions of materialism, peace and social progress, but policy in science is still made by the ruling class—the reactionary monopoly bourgeoisie.

Scientific and Technical Revolution
and Its Social Impact

We are witnessing the *development of the scientific and technical revolution* caused by the enormous progress in automation, radioelectronics and telemechanics, by the use of atomic energy, exploration of outer space, and breakthroughs in cybernetics, chemistry, physics, biology and other sciences.

The scientific and technical revolution embraces not only science and technology, but also *production*. Profound qualitative changes take place in the equipment and technology of production and its energy base. The character of labour also changes, becoming more and more intellectual. The progress of science and technology, cybernetics in the first place, makes it possible to mechanise and automate physical as well as certain types of mental labour. Cultural and professional standards and the qualification of the workers are growing.

The significance of the scientific and technical revolution is so immense that not a single more or less important event in modern history can be understood without a searching analysis of that revolution and mainly of its *social consequences*.

In our day scientific and technical progress has become one of the main arenas of the struggle and competition of the two opposing social systems—socialism and capitalism. "Those who have the greatest technical equipment, organisation and discipline, and the best machines, will gain the upper hand,"* said Lenin. He did not consider it possible to build socialism without mastering science and technology.

Fulfilling Lenin's behests the CPSU promotes the development of science and technology, it sees to it that science is introduced into diverse fields of social life and that fuller use is made of the opportunities opened by scientific and technical progress to accelerate economic growth and meet the requirements of all members of society.

The main impellent of scientific and technical progress under capitalism are *profit and bitter rivalry.* It is the quest for profits, the desire to vanquish their rivals on the market that compels capitalists to promote science and on its basis improve technology and engineering. Capitalists in the USA, Britain, FRG, Japan and other highly industrialised countries astutely use scientific and technological achievements to increase production, raise labour productivity, improve the quality of production and so forth. In this respect it would be a grave mistake to underestimate scientific and technological progress in these countries and even more so to ignore their experience in implementing it in production, inasmuch as this experience can and ought to be applied under socialism, but, needless to say, with due consideration for the qualitative specifics of the socialist economy.

At the same time there are glaring contradictions in scientific and technical progress in capitalist society, where science and technology are instruments of exploitation. It is not accidental, therefore, that imperialism often dooms science and engineering to a one-sided development, for the monopolists are concerned mainly with developing those branches of science which spell greater profits. One of their priorities is to expand branches of the war industry, for arms production is the most lucrative business. Militarisation is a characteristic and very dangerous aspect of science and technology in contemporary capitalist society.

Thanks to progress in science and engineering capitalist production expands, while the purchasing power of the population is limited, and sales on foreign markets are impeded by rivalry. New machines and mechanisms drive masses of working people out of the sphere of production, and unemployment increases. As a result, the purchasing power falls and scientific and technical progress is slowed down. Anarchy and rivalry give rise to commercial secrets in science and this, too, stands in the way of

---

* V.I. Lenin, "Extraordinary Fourth All-Russia Congress of Soviets. March 14-16, 1918", *Collected Works*, Vol. 27, p. 195.

scientific and technical cooperation and leads to parallelism in research. The monopolies shelve thousands of important inventions and discoveries until their "commercial value" rises.

The scientific and technical revolution under socialism has totally different objectives, prospects and consequences. It affirms the planned organisation of production in order to ensure the wellbeing and all-round development of all members of society. That is why socialism and communism give ample room for the advance of the scientific and technical revolution and use the achievements of science and technology in the interests of the people and not to their detriment. "We Communists proceed from the belief that the scientific and technical revolution acquires a true orientation consistent with the interests of man and society only under socialism," states the Report of the CPSU Central Committee to the 25th CPSU Congress. "In turn, the end objectives of the social revolution, the building of a communist society, can only be attained on the basis of accelerated scientific and technical progress."*

In socialist society science is an important means of developing production and raising the material and cultural standards of the working people. The natural sciences play a decisive role in technical progress and in the development of production skills of the working people, and enhance their cultural and technical level. The social sciences are also very important. By equipping people with knowledge of the laws of the functioning and development of society, they constitute the scientific foundation for directing economic and social processes and play a great part in the communist education of the people and in fostering a dialectical-materialistic outlook. Under socialism science is a mighty weapon of peace, creativity and unprecedented social progress.

Another distinguishing feature of Soviet science is its *profound kinship with the people.* This kinship manifests itself not only in the fact that science serves the people, but also in that the people have gained wide access to science. Hundreds of thousands of Soviet scientists come from the very midst of the people to whom they dedicate all their strength amd knowledge. Together with the scientists millions of innovators of production, inventors and rationalisers ensure the progress of Soviet science.

The socialist system enables society to conduct research according to a general state plan and to coordinate the work of numerous scientific institutions so that scientists can concentrate on the most important problems. The dialectical-materialistic outlook prevailing in socialist society rids sci-

---

* *Documents and Resolutions. XXVth Congress of the CPSU,* pp. 56-57.

ence of the morbid influence of idealism and religion and equips scientists with the only truly scientific methodology of studying natural and social processes.

As socialist construction continues, science draws ever closer to production, which in its turn more and more extensively draws upon scientific achievements. *Science is increasingly turning into a genuine productive force.*

The Scientific and Technological Revolution and Nature

The scientific and technological revolution has taken place not only in the social, but also in the natural environment and its influence on the latter has been enormous. Through science and technology man transforms nature for his own purposes and interests and these transformations in terms of their scope, speed and intensity are simply incomparable with the transformations that occur spontaneously in nature. In an exceptionally short time by geological standards artificial seas have been made, rivers turned back and mountains of waste rock built. The result of this has been a sharp and at times irreversible upsetting of the ecological balance and the normal flow of natural processes.

Nature is the cradle of man and mankind, the primary source of all the wealth that has been created by human labour. Nature is our friend and our eternal and irreplaceable companion in both life and labour, but it will not allow a thoughtless, and even more, a barbaric attitude towards itself. Nature takes its revenge on man if he tries to transform it with no thought for its laws. It can deprive him of raw materials, energy and food and without these his own existence is unthinkable.

A century ago Engels observed* that we should not flatter ourselves on account of our human victories over nature, because for every such victory it would take revenge. It is true that each of these victories at first gave the expected results, but subsequently they have had completely unforeseen consequences which have not infrequently destroyed all the benefits that were first gained. For example, the unreasonable exploitation of the land at first brings good harvests but later leads to soil erosion and aridity; a powerful hydroelectric power station provides needed energy, but the reservoirs that feed it often cause swamps over vast areas, the destruction of aquatic life and severely restrict or even stop shipping. We must be extremely thoughtful in our attitude to nature, or we may not avoid drastic

---

* See Frederick Engels, *Dialectics of Nature*, Progress Publishers, Moscow, 1974, p. 180

consequences. Nature should not be conquered, it must be *scientifically controlled*.

Man's attitude to nature largely depends on the social system in which he lives.

Capitalism exploits nature mercilessly, crippling it in the name of the holy of holies, profit. Socialism makes it possible to conserve and improve nature. These possibilities, however, are far from being always and everywhere realised. Woods are chopped down thoughtlessly, and yet they are the most important suppliers of oxygen and atmospheric humidity. Industrial, energy and road construction often result in the destruction of enormous areas of arable land. Lakes and rivers become polluted. The air we breathe becomes polluted, too. It is highly important to stop these practices and conserve nature for future generations, and improve and beautify it. The rational use of natural resources and environmental protection are an important aspect of the economic policy of the CPSU and the Soviet state, being the sacred duty of all Soviet people according to the Constitution of the USSR.

The Soviet people are building a new society. Nature in that society must be as beautiful as the society itself and the people who live in it. Science and technology have an enormous creative role to play, especially since under socialism science is closely tied up with production—the universal form of interaction between man and nature. Production, in its turn, makes increasing use of scientific discoveries. Thus *science is more and more being transformed into a direct social productive force*.

The Transformation of Science into a Productive Force

The transformation of science into a direct productive force does not mean that it is becoming a new and independent element of the productive forces alongside the means of production and people who are employed in production. Science performs the role of a productive force only through *technology and people*.

How does the role played by science as a productive force manifest itself?

Firstly, scientific achievements are embodied in *advanced equipment and technology*. Today whole industries (nuclear energy, polymer chemistry, microbiology, electronics, etc.) are products of science and cannot exist without it. Production is increasingly turning into the technological application of science, a materialised force of knowledge, a gigantic laboratory where the latest scientific achievements are brought to completion, verified and applied.

Secondly, scientific achievements become *embodied in the producer, in his knowledge, skill and professional experience.* Modern comprehensive mechanisation, let alone automation, fill labour with an intellectual content and demand that a worker has high cultural, technical and professional standards. By equipping him with modern knowledge, science enhances his skill, raises labour productivity and turns him into an active rationaliser and inventor.

Thirdly, *research work is making ever deeper inroads into the sphere of material production and is turning into productive work.* Research is conducted on an increasing scale at numerous research and design institutes, laboratories and departments at factories, and at collective and state farms. In a word, science is turning into one of the basic elements of modern production.

When we say that science is turning into a direct production force this applies in the first place to mechanics, physics, chemistry, biology and other natural and technical sciences. At the same time social sciences, particularly economic sciences, are coming to play an increasing role in production. With the aid of mathematical methods and electronic computers, these sciences help to improve production management and pave the way for the most effective utilisation of material, labour and financial resources which is particularly important in view of the vast scale of contemporary production. And that is not to mention the great role played by social sciences in moulding the inner make-up of the workers and their outlook.

Science's organic links with production should not be assessed only from the point of view of its direct use and scientists should not be required promptly to apply their discoveries in production. The purpose of science is not only to find solutions to urgent problems, but to build up a "reserve" for the future, solve vital theoretical problems which pave the way for social progress and discover new roads in science and technology.

Science as an important sphere of social life is developing at a rapid pace. The number of researchers and research institutions is increasing. Expenditures on science grow faster than the national income and industrial production.

Science in the USSR has made great progress thanks to concern displayed by the people, the Party and the Soviet Government. The achievements in the exploration of outer space offer striking proof of this.

But Soviet science has by no means exhausted its possibilities. That is why the Party and Government work tirelessly to improve the system of planning, direction and stimulation of scientific research and to augment the economic and social effectivity of science. Special attention is focussed on strengthening and extending the bonds between science and production, establishing research and production associations and complex scientific institutions whose task is to conduct the full volume of research, design and production work, including the batch output of new products and the establishment of research institutes at large industrial and other enterprises. The strengthening of the planning principle is a prime prerequisite for heightening the effectivity of scientific research and the speediest practical application of its results.

The revolution in the development of the productive forces started off by science will become increasingly significant and profound. Hence the task *organically to fuse the achievements of the scientific and technical revolution with the advantages of the socialist economic system,* to unfold more broadly intrinsically socialist forms of fusing science with production.

Conclusion

By mid-19th century, capitalism had replaced feudalism in many countries. Together with it the proletariat, the most progressive and consistently revolutionary class whose mission was to put an end to exploitation of man by man and establish a new, communist society, emerged on the historical scene. The proletariat's liberation movement confronted science with the exceptionally important tasks of formulating a scientific theory that would help it accomplish its historic mission and become its ideological, weapon in the fight against capitalism, for socialism and communism. Science fulfilled this insistent demand of history: the brilliant leaders of the working class and of all working people, Marx and Engels, evolved Marxism whose component and theoretical foundation is Marxist philosophy—dialectical and historical materialism.

Marxist-Leninist philosophy is the sole scientific theory and method of cognising and explaining reality. It proves beyond all doubt that by its very nature the world is material, that everything in it changes, develops and inexorably moves forward, from the lower to the higher, from the old to the new. Presenting as it does a true picture of the world and disclosing the more general laws of development of nature and society, Marxist philosophy is a mighty instrument of revolutionary action. It reflects history's objective dialectics and is the theoretical foundation of the strategy and tactics of the Marxist parties. The main demands of dialectical materialism which guide Marxist parties in their titanic work of the revolutionary reorganisation of the world are to conduct a trenchant analysis of the contradictions of social development, to be able to disclose and cope with these contradictions in good time and in the interests of historical progress, to approach the solution of crucial social problems from concrete historical positions and to be able to discern in life all that is new, to rely upon it and to secure its triumph. Marxist philosophy is the keenest theoretical weapon of the working class in its struggle against bourgeois ideology, revisionism and dogmatism, nationalism and sectarianism.

Marxist-Leninist philosophy is a living, creative teaching. It does not stand still, but constantly moves forward keeping abreast of the changing life and enriching itself with scientific achievements and socio-historical practice. Lenin upheld and developed Marxist philosophy in conditions of an unexampled social change, humanity's transition from capitalism to socialism, in conditions of the latest revolution in natural science. Today the victorious banner of creative Marxism is held aloft by the Communist Party of the Soviet Union and Marxist parties in other countries.

Marx's teaching is all-powerful because of its truth, Lenin wrote. The great truth of Marxism has been confirmed by life, by the greatest revolution ever to take place in the world and the socialist reorganisation of society. The rise and development of the world socialist system, the complete and final victory of socialism in the USSR, mankind's inexorable advance towards the bright communist morrow, convincingly attest to the triumph of the mighty ideas of Marxism-Leninism. The new historical epoch witnessed the full triumph of the proletariat's revolutionary look. Marxism-Leninism dominates the thoughts of progressive humanity.

Socialism's gains are enormous and undeniable. But it should not be forgotten that capitalism still exists in many countries. And by no means the last role in keeping it alive is played by the reactionary ideology of the contemporary bourgeoisie which does all it can to whitewash capitalism and defer the death sentence which history has pronounced upon it. The current bitter struggle between communist and bourgeois ideologies will be won by communist ideology. Behind it is the truth of life, and truth is invincible. This great truth are the ideals of communism which are winning the minds and hearts of all honest people in the world. As regards bourgeois ideology, it has not passed the test of history. Its downfall is just as inevitable as the demise of the social system which it represents.

Mankind has discerned the real image of capitalism and does not want and will not tolerate its further existence. Moribund capitalism will be replaced by the new and most just society—communism. Such is the objective law of social development, such is the objective dialectics of history.